pathfinder® guide

Lancashire

WALKS

Compiled by
Brian Conduit

JARROLD
publishing

Acknowledgements
My thanks for the valuable advice and numerous useful
leaflets that I obtained from the various tourist information
centres throughout the area.

Text:	Brian Conduit
Photography:	Brian Conduit
Editor:	Crawford Gillan
Designers:	Doug Whitworth
	Ellen Moorcraft

Series Consultant: Brian Conduit

Jarrold Publishing   ISBN 0-7117-2084-3

While every care has been taken to ensure the accuracy of
the route directions, the publishers cannot accept
responsibility for errors or omissions, or for changes in
details given. The countryside is not static: hedges and
fences can be removed, field boundaries can be altered,
footpaths can be rerouted and changes in ownership can
result in the closure or diversion of some concessionary
paths. Also, paths that are easy and pleasant for walking in
fine conditions may become slippery, muddy and difficult in
wet weather, while stepping-stones across rivers and streams
may become impassable.
    If you find an inaccuracy in either the text or maps, please
write to Jarrold Publishing at one of the addresses below.

First published 2002
by Jarrold Publishing

Printed in Belgium
by Proost NV, Turnhout. 1/02

Jarrold Publishing
Pathfinder Guides, Whitefriars, Norwich NR3 1TR
E-mail: pathfinder@jarrold.com
www.jarrold-publishing.co.uk/pathfinders

Front cover: Crook o'Lune
Previous page: Lancaster Castle

Contents

Contents

Short, easy walks

Walks of modest length, likely to involve some modest uphill walking

More challenging walks which may be longer and/or over more rugged terrain, often with some stiff climbs

HEYSHAM to
Douglas   4 hrs
Belfast   4 hrs

FLEETWOOD to
Larne   8 hrs

SCALE 1:384 615 or 1 INCH to about 6 MILES *1CM to 3.8KM*

0   2   4   6   8   10 KILOMETRES   15

0   2   4   6 MILES   8   10

KEYMAP HEIGHTS SHOWN IN FEET

MORECAMBE BAY

THE FYLDE

ULVERSTON
BARROW-IN-FURNESS
DALTON-IN-FURNESS
GRANGE-OVER-SANDS
KIRKBY LONS
CARNFORTH
MORECAMBE
HEYSHAM
LANCASTER
FLEETWOOD
CLEVELEYS
THORNTON
POULTON-LE-FYLDE
BLACKPOOL
KIRKHAM
FRECKLETON
LYTHAM ST ANNE'S
ST ANNES
WARTON
PRESTON
BLACKB
BAMBER BRIDGE
FULWOOD
LONGRIDGE
LEYLAND
SOUTHPORT
CHORLEY
ADLINGTON
COPPULL
STANDISH
BURSCOUGH BRIDGE
ORMSKIRK
SKELMERSDALE
FORMBY
WIGAN
WESTHOUGH
INCE-IN-MAKERFIELD
ABRAM
HINDL
BILLINGE
ASHTON-IN-MAKERFIELD
GOLBORNE
ST HELENS
HAYDOCK
NEWTON-LE-WILLOWS
PRESCOT
KNOWSLEY
BOOTLE
WALLASEY

Keymap

At-a-glance...

Walk	Page	Start	Nat. Grid Reference	Distance	Time
Anglezarke, White Coppice and Great Hill	87	Anglezarke Car Park	SD619161	9 miles (14.5 km)	5 hrs
Barrowford and Roughlee	32	Barrowford	SD863398	4 miles (6.4 km)	2 hrs
Caton Footpath and the River Lune	14	Crook o'Lune Picnic Site	SD522658	3½ miles (5.6km)	1½hrs
Crawshawbooth and Lumb	65	Crawshawbooth	SD810252	7 miles (11.3km)	3½hrs
Darwen Moor	38	Roddlesworth	SD665215	4 miles (1.6km)	2 hrs
Douglas Valley and Ashurst's Beacon	71	Beacon Country Park	SD504504	8 miles (12.9km)	4 hrs
Formby Point	18	Formby Point	SD276067	4 miles (6.4km)	2 hrs
Foulridge – Reservoir and Canal	20	Foulridge Wharf	SD889427	4 miles (6.4km)	2 hrs
Gorple Road and Towneley Park	52	Hurstwood	SD883313	6 miles (9.7km)	3 hrs
Haigh Hall and the Leeds and Liverpool Canal	16	Haigh Country Park	SD597084	3½miles (5.6km)	2 hrs
Hodder and Dunsop Valleys	74	Dunsop Bridge	SD661501	7½miles (12.1km)	4 hrs
Holcombe Moor and the Peel Tower	62	Ramsbottom Market Place	SD791170	6½miles (10.5km)	3½hrs
Jumbles Country Park to Hall i'th Wood	55	Jumbles Country Park Info Centre	SD737139	6½miles (10.5km)	3½hrs
Lune Estuary and the Lancaster Canal	84	Lancaster Castle	SD475618	11 miles (17.5km)	5 hrs
Lune Valley – Kirkby Lonsdale to Whittington	42	Kirkby Lonsdale	SD616783	6¼miles (10.1km)	3 hrs
Lytham and the Ribble Estuary	59	Lytham	SD378269	7½miles (12.1km)	3½hrs
Parbold Hill and The Fairy Glen	49	Parbold	SD491107	6 miles (9.7km)	3 hrs
Parlick and Fair Snape Fell	81	Fell Foot	SD602442	5½miles (8.9km)	3½hrs
Pilling	40	Pilling Car Park	SD464484	5½miles (8.9km)	2½hrs
Poulton–Le–Fylde and Skippool Creek	26	Poulton-Le-Fylde	SD621161	5 miles (8 km)	2½hrs
Ribchester, Stonyhurst and the River Ribble	77	Ribchester	SD647352	9½miles (15.3km)	5 hrs
Sankey Valley	12	Sankey Valley Country Park	SY577945	3½miles (5.6km)	1½hrs
Scorton, Grize Dale and Nicky Nook	68	Scorton Picnic Site	SD507067	6½miles (10.5km)	3½hrs
Silverdale and Arnside Tower	24	Silverdale	SD467748	4½miles (7.2km)	2 hrs
Slaidburn and Newton	29	Slaidburn	SD714524	5 miles (8 km)	2½hrs
Whalley, River Calder and Read Park	35	Spring Wood Picnic Site	SD744359	5½miles (8.9km)	3 hrs
Worsley and the Bridgewater Canal	22	Worsley	SD748004	5 miles (8.9km)	2½hrs
The Yealands and Leighton Hall	45	Tewitfield Locks	SD520736	6½miles (10.5km)	3 hrs

Comments

A mainly woodland and reservoir walk leads to the picturesque hamlet of White Coppice. This is followed by a steady climb over the bare expanses of Great Hill, with superb moorland views.

Attractive waterside walking is combined with grand views of Pendle Hill and a village that has connections with the Pendle witches.

An opening stretch along a former railway track is followed by a riverside walk beside the meandering Lune. There are superb views over the valley.

Some rough moorland walking gives you fine and extensive views across the Rossendale moors. Near the start you pass a historic chapel.

The contrasting views from Darwen Tower take in the mills of Blackburn and Darwen and the open expanses of the West Pennine Moors.

From a ridge top start, the route descends into the Douglas valley for a walk beside the Leeds and Liverpool Canal. A steady climb leads back onto the ridge and a fine viewpoint.

This fine walk on the Merseyside coast embraces pine woods, dunes, a long sandy beach and views of Liverpool and the coast of North Wales.

After an opening walk along the shores of a reservoir, paths and tracks lead across fields and through woodland to the towpath of the Leeds and Liverpool Canal.

The route descends from the open moorland to the east of Burnley into the gentler surroundings of Towneley Park, with an opportunity to visit the hall.

An old hall, an attractive stretch of canal and fine woodlands make up a varied and interesting walk on the edge of Wigan.

This exhilarating walk in the Forest of Bowland gives you superb views over the Bowland fells and the beautiful Hodder and Dunsop valleys .

An opening stretch beside the River Irwell and a steady climb through a wooded valley is followed by an exhilarating walk across Holcombe Moor to the Peel Tower.

Two historic houses are passed on this varied walk near Bolton. It starts at a popular country park based around a reservoir and includes moorland, and a steep, wooded valley.

This long but mostly flat walk takes you along the Lune estuary from the centre of Lancaster to Conder Green. Most of the return is beside the Lancaster Canal.

This is a superb riverside walk beside the Lune and on no account must you miss the magnificent Ruskin's View at Kirkby Lonsdale.

Lytham is an attractive starting point and there are wide views over both the Fylde countryside and the Ribble estuary.

There is attractive canalside and riverside walking, a wooded ravine and extensive views over the West Lancashire coastal plain.

A short steep climb up Parlick is followed by a lengthier but steadier ascent of the adjacent Fair Snape Fell. Both summits are magnificent viewpoints.

Much of the second half of the walk is along an embankment above Morecambe Bay and there are superb views across to the Bowland fells and Lakeland mountains.

This is a flat and easy walk in the Fylde and the middle section takes you along the attractive shore of the Wyre estuary.

Throughout this lengthy walk in the Ribble valley, there are fine views of the valley and Pendle Hill, attractive woodland and riverside walking and considerable historic interest.

This short and pleasant walk includes a stroll along one of the earliest canals and a view of one of the first railway viaducts.

The highlights of this route are the beautiful walk through Grize Dale followed by the brief and easy ascent to the summit of Nicky Nook, a magnificent viewpoint.

There is attractive woodland, fine views across the expanses of Morecambe Bay and the route passes by a ruined medieval peel tower.

You enjoy a succession of superb views over the Bowland fells and Hodder valley and the walk ends with a stroll beside the Hodder.

Medieval church, ancient crosses, ruined abbey, two imposing Victorian railway viaducts and grand views over the Ribble and Calder valleys make up a varied and highly scenic walk.

There is much historic interest on this walk which utilises a former railway track and the towpath of the first great canal of the Industrial Revolution.

An opening stretch beside the Lancaster canal is followed by superb woodland walking, magnificent views of both Ingleborough and the Lakeland mountains, villages and an interesting house.

At-a-glance...

Introduction to Lancashire

The tiny and remote Lancashire village of Dunsop Bridge has a claim to fame that perhaps few people outside the area know. The telephone kiosk there records that it is the nearest settlement to the exact geographical centre of Great Britain, deemed by the Ordnance Survey to be at an uninhabited spot a few miles away. Dunsop Bridge is situated amidst the glorious countryside of the Forest of Bowland and for a county more associated with mill chimneys and cobbled streets – an image created in the popular mind as a result of school history lessons on the Industrial Revolution, the drawings of L.S.Lowry and *Coronation Street* – there is much fine and varied scenery to enjoy. Indeed, there can be few counties that possess such a range of landscapes, from the Fen-like lowlands of the West Lancashire coastal plain to the Highland-like majesty of the Bowland Fells, and from the lush greenery of the Ribble and Lune valleys to the bare bleakness of the West Pennine Moors. Added to this is an impressive collection of historic monuments and some very attractive villages.

Greater Manchester and Merseyside

This walking guide includes those areas of Greater Manchester and Merseyside that lie to the north of the River Mersey as these were part of the traditional county of Lancashire, before the local government changes in 1974. Although these are the most heavily industrialised and urbanised parts of the region, they are not devoid of good walking and attractive countryside, especially as much of the heavy industry has gone and the coal mines have disappeared. The Pennine moorlands sweep down almost to the outskirts of Manchester itself and the Merseyside coast between Liverpool and Southport, a coastline of sand dunes, pine woods and wide flat beaches, has one of the finest dune systems in the country.

Coastal Lancashire

A journey through Lancashire reveals its tremendous scenic variety. Starting with the coastal areas, in the north west corner is a region of wooded limestone hills fringing the shores of Morecambe Bay. This is the Arnside and Silverdale Area of Outstanding Natural Beauty, shared with neighbouring Cumbria. It is honeycombed with public footpaths and a superb walking area. Between the Lune and Ribble estuaries is the flat and fertile country of the Fylde. This is usually associated with the popular coastal resorts of Blackpool, Cleveleys, St Anne's and Lytham but there are stretches of unspoilt coastline and estuary and, inland, plenty of pleasant footpaths and attractive villages to explore. South of the Ribble estuary are the reclaimed marshes and mosses of the West Lancashire coastal plain, now a major market gardening region, which extends down to the Mersey estuary and the outskirts of Liverpool.

Inland Lancashire

Inland, the Lancashire landscape, even when viewed from the coast, is dominated by the line of the Pennines and their various westerly outliers. One such outlying mass is the Forest of Bowland. In the Middle Ages this was a royal hunting forest and it remains one of the loneliest and most sparsely inhabited stretches of country

River Douglas and Parbold Hill

anywhere in England. The scenery is superb – rolling moorlands, deep sided valleys, tiny hamlets and isolated farms – with extensive views in places over the Fylde and across Morecambe Bay to the line of the Lakeland fells. Large areas of Bowland are without public rights of way but access agreements have opened up some of the finest moorland areas and most of the outstanding peaks to walkers.

To the north, the Bowland Fells are bordered by the beautiful Lune valley, one of Lancashire's gems. On the south, they dip down to the Hodder – surely the county's loveliest river and a tributary of the Ribble, a fine introduction to the more gentle scenic delights of the beautiful Ribble valley. The Ribble flows between the Bowland Fells to the north and Pendle Hill to the south. The latter, possibly Lancashire's most distinctive landmark, is particularly associated with the witch trials of the early 17th century. In 1612 a group of women from the Pendle area were put on trial for witchcraft, found guilty and hanged at Lancaster Castle. Further south are the bare moorlands and deep-sided cloughs of the Forest of Rossendale and West Pennine Moors, more superb walking country. Two outlying hills, Parbold Hill and Ashurst's Beacon, thrust westwards towards the coastal

Towneley Hall

plain and the rolling Pennine moors continue southwards, reaching to the edges of the urban and industrial belt around Manchester.

History

Up until the Industrial Revolution, Lancashire was a sparsely populated county, mainly occupied with farming, quarrying and small-scale cottage textile industry. Towns were few and far between. Even Lancaster, the county town and seat of a great castle, remained relatively small until the late 17th century when it began to develop as an important trans-Atlantic port. Over the next century it flourished and its heyday is reflected in the legacy of fine Georgian architecture. During the 19th century Lancaster declined, partly as a result of the silting–up of the Lune and partly because of its comparative isolation from the main centres of industry and population, which were rapidly developing in the south of the county.

It was in the narrow gritstone valleys of the Pennines that the textile industry developed, aided by sheep farming on the adjacent slopes, a damp climate, fast flowing streams, local coal supplies and the proximity of the port of Liverpool, important both for the importing of raw cotton from America and the exporting of the finished product. A series of inventions, mainly by local men, transformed the cotton industry in the 18th century and put it in the forefront of the Industrial Revolution. Manchester became

the main centre and Liverpool the chief port and scores of towns –
Blackburn, Preston, Burnley, Bolton, Oldham, Rochdale etc. – became
major cotton manufacturing centres. Such was the importance of 'King
Cotton' to Britain's trade and prosperity in the Victorian era that the phrase
'England's bread hangs by Lancashire's thread' was coined.

Industrial growth spawned transport developments and it was in
Lancashire that the country's earliest canals – the St Helens and
Bridgewater Canals – and the first passenger railway – between Liverpool
and Manchester – were built. Later canals were the Leeds and Liverpool,
constructed to link Lancashire and the Mersey with the woollen towns of
Yorkshire on the other side of the Pennines, and the Lancaster Canal, built
in a vain attempt to prolong Lancaster's prosperity as a port. These canals
are among the most enduring and attractive legacies of the Industrial
Revolution era and their towpaths – featured prominently in this guide –
provide pleasant and trouble-free walking.

At the height of the Industrial Revolution, Lancashire also became a
popular holiday destination. Railway links between the teeming cotton
manufacturing towns and the coast, coupled with some fine sandy beaches,
led to the rise of the resorts of Morecambe, Southport, Lytham St Anne's
and especially Blackpool.

Walking in Lancashire

A misleading image and close proximity to three of Britain's national parks
has led to Lancashire being somewhat underrated as a walking area and
many walking enthusiasts tend to pass through on their way to the Lake
District, Yorkshire Dales or Peak District. They are missing out on much
fine and varied scenery and first-time visitors to the county may well be
agreeably surprised by what it has to offer. Lancashire has a number of
long-distance paths. Foremost is the Ribble Way which follows the river
from its mouth to its source. The Pendle Way, Rossendale Way and Burnley
Way provide well-waymarked circular routes in those regions of the county
and the Lancashire Coastal Way and Sefton Coastal Path make up an
almost continuous coastal route from the Mersey to the Cumbrian border.

The obvious and most popular areas for walkers are the Forest of
Bowland, Ribble and Lune valleys, Pennine moors and the Silverdale area,
near the Cumbrian border. Walks have also been included, however, in the
flatter country of the Fylde and West Lancashire, along the Merseyside
coast and in the more built-up area, near Manchester, to provide contrast
and variety.

Enjoy the footpaths and bridleways, the moorlands and river valleys and
the coast and canal towpaths of one of England's most varied and
distinctive counties. There is much for the walker – whether it is
challenging hill and moorland hikes or more gentle lowland strolls – to
sample.

Sankey Valley

Start	Sankey Valley Country Park, Bradleigh Lock car park, signposted from road between Earlestown and Vulcan Village
Distance	3½ miles (5.6km)
Approximate time	1½ hours
Parking	Bradleigh Lock
Refreshments	Pub just before point (C)
Ordnance Survey maps	Landranger 108 (Liverpool, Southport & Wigan), Explorer 276 (Bolton, Wigan & Warrington)

This short and easy walk takes you through the pleasant, open countryside of the Sankey valley, once a busy industrial area, between St Helens, Newton-le-Willows and Warrington. There are wide views, the route twice crosses Sankey Brook and the final 1 mile (1.6km) is beside the disused Sankey (or St Helens) Canal, allegedly the oldest canal in the country.

The Sankey Valley Country Park, an invaluable 'green corridor' of grassland, woodland, water features and open views, follows the course of the Sankey Canal for 15 miles (24km) from St Helens, through Warrington to the River Mersey at Widnes. There is a Canal Trail for walkers and cyclists and there are plans for the restoration of navigation on the canal.

From the car park, turn right alongside the canal, turn left to cross

Christmas card scene in the Sankey valley

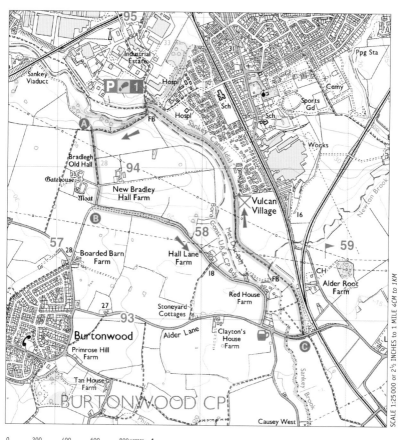

| 0 | 200 | 400 | 600 | 800 METRES | 1 |
| 0 | 200 | 400 | 600 YARDS | ½ | KILOMETRES MILES |

the swing bridge over it and keep ahead through trees to cross a footbridge over Sankey Brook. The path bends right and heads gently uphill above the brook to a T-junction Ⓐ. Turn left and continue along a straight track across fields. From this track there are impressive views of Sankey Viaduct, built by George and Robert Stephenson in 1830 to carry the first passenger railway in the world – between Liverpool and Manchester – across the valley. A little farther on you pass the buildings of Bradleigh Hall on the right, where the 15th-century gatehouse of the former moated medieval manor house remains.

Keep ahead at a crossroads of tracks to reach a lane and turn left Ⓑ along this narrow, winding, pleasantly tree-lined lane to a road. Cross over, turn left and re-cross Sankey Brook. In front of the next bridge Ⓒ, descend steps and, at the bottom, turn left to pass under the bridge and keep ahead along a track. After crossing Hey Lock, the route continues along the left bank of the Sankey Canal. This disputes with the Bridgewater Canal in the claim to be the first real canal of the Industrial Revolution. It is certainly slightly earlier – opened in 1757 – and was constructed to carry coal from the area around St Helens to the Mersey. Over to the right, Vulcan Village can be seen, based around an iron foundry and once home to a major rubber industry. Follow the attractive canalside path back to the starting point of the walk at the Sankey Valley car park.　　●

SCALE 1:25 000 or 2½ INCHES to 1 MILE 4CM to 1KM

Caton Footpath and the River Lune

Start	Crook o'Lune Picnic Site, 1½ miles (2.4km) east of Caton
Distance	3½ miles (5.6km)
Approximate time	1½ hours
Parking	Crook o'Lune
Refreshments	Pubs and café at Caton
Ordnance Survey maps	Landranger 97 (Kendal & Morecambe, Windermere & Lancaster), Outdoor Leisure 41 (Forest of Bowland & Ribblesdale)

The first part of this flat and easy walk in the Lune valley is along a disused railway track. The rest is across meadows beside the meandering River Lune. There are fine views of the valley and the surrounding hills, especially at the start where you enjoy the classic view from the Crook o'Lune. Near the end, Artle Beck has to be forded by stepping stones, which may be difficult after heavy or prolonged rain. If the beck is running high and the stones are covered by water, simply retrace your steps.

Crook o'Lune

From the car park there is the classic view over the Lune, painted by Turner (1816-18). Start by facing the river, turn right and descend steps to a tarmac path. Turn left, in the Caton direction, cross a former railway bridge over the Lune and continue along the straight tarmac path. This path – the Caton Footpath – has been created from the track of a railway which ran between Lancaster and Wennington. Opened in 1849, it was never successful and finally closed in the 1960s.

On reaching a track, turn right if you want to visit Caton – shops, pubs and café. Otherwise, keep ahead along the Caton Footpath, crossing a bridge over Artle Beck, as far as a tarmac track where the path almost emerges onto the road. Turn left along the track (A) and, after climbing a stile, the route continues along a rough, hedge-lined track which curves left towards the river. Climb a stile, keep ahead to climb two more stiles in quick succession and continue along the track beside the Lune. After climbing the next stile, the route keeps along the edge of riverside meadows and over a series of stiles, following the Lune around a sharp left bend, passing a waterworks bridge (B) and crossing the stepping stones over Artle Beck, a most attractive part of the walk.

After passing under the disused railway bridge near the end, keep ahead to climb a stile in front of a road bridge and continue to a public footpath sign by a gate onto the road. Turn sharp left here onto a tarmac path, go through a gate and turn left to rejoin the Caton Footpath. Recross the bridge to return to the start.

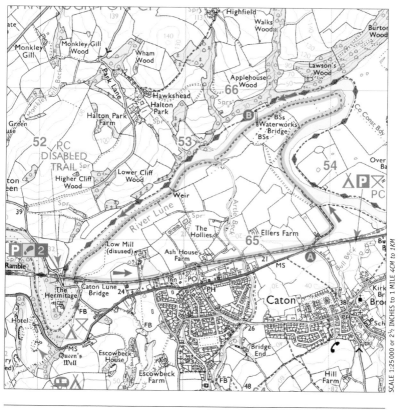

Haigh Hall and the Leeds and Liverpool Canal

Start	Haigh Country Park
Distance	3½ miles (5.6km)
Approximate time	2 hours
Parking	Haigh Country Park
Refreshments	Café at the Country Park, pub near point (D)
Ordnance Survey maps	Landrangers 108 (Liverpool, Southport & Wigan) and 109 (Manchester, Bolton & Warrington), Explorer 276 (Bolton, Wigan & Warrington)

In the quiet woodlands of Haigh Country Park and by the peaceful banks of the Leeds and Liverpool Canal, it is hard to believe that this was once a busy industrial area and that the town centre of Wigan is barely 2 miles (3.2km) away. From the terrace of Haigh Hall, there are extensive views across Wigan and the Douglas valley to Parbold Hill and Ashurst's Beacon.

Haigh Hall was built in the 19th century for the Earls of Crawford, who owned nearby coal mines and an iron foundry. It is now the focal point of a country park and in the former stables and coach house there is an exhibition area, shop and café. The Earls of Crawford were also responsible for the planting of the extensive woodlands that are such an attractive feature of the park.

The walk starts on the terrace in front of Haigh Hall, from where there is a fine view across Wigan and the Douglas valley. Facing the view, turn right and right again along the side of the hall and, at a T-junction, turn left along a gently ascending tarmac drive.

The drive curves gradually right to go through the gates of the park onto a lane. Bear right along the tree-lined Copperas Lane and, at a public footpath sign, turn right over a stile **A**.

Haigh Hall

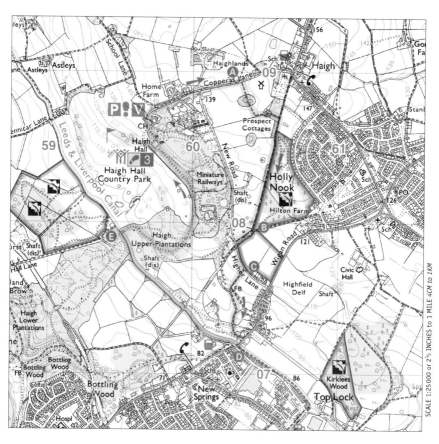

SCALE 1:25 000 or 2½ INCHES to 1 MILE 4CM to 1KM

```
0    200   400   600   800 METRES  1
                                    KILOMETRES
0    200   400   600 YARDS    ½     MILES
```

Walk across a field – there is a former windmill to the left – towards a circle of trees, continue through them, passing between two pools, and continue across the field to the far side where you turn left along its right edge. Climb a stile in the corner and keep ahead along a narrow path in front of the gardens of cottages which turns left to a track. Turn right to reach a T-junction and turn right again onto an attractive, mainly tree-lined enclosed path which heads gently downhill to a T-junction by a kissing gate on the left **B**.

Turn right along a path – it soon becomes a tarmac track – to a lane, turn left to cross a bridge over a disused railway and, at a public footpath sign,

turn right onto an enclosed path **C**. The path descends gently, bears left to cross a brook and continues to a track. Turn left, pass beside a gate and follow the winding track to a road. Turn right, cross a bridge over the canal, turn left into Withington Lane and, almost immediately, turn left again to the towpath of the Leeds and Liverpool Canal **D**.

Turn left to pass under the bridge and keep beside the canal as far as a cast iron bridge (No. 60). In front of the bridge, turn left up steps, turn right to cross it **E** and continue along a tarmac track through the delightful woodlands of the Haigh Plantations. Take the right-hand track at a fork and the track ascends and curves gradually left to emerge from the trees. Follow it back to Haigh Hall. ●

Formby Point

Start	Formby Point, Lifeboat Road car park and picnic site
Distance	4 miles (6.4km)
Approximate time	2 hours
Parking	Formby Point
Refreshments	None
Ordnance Survey maps	Landranger 108 (Liverpool, Southport & Wigan), Explorer 285 (Southport & Chorley)

The first part of the walk is through or along the edge of woodland which fringes the dunes of Formby Point on the Merseyside coast. It continues over the dunes to the beach and this is followed by an exhilarating 1½ mile (2.4km) walk along the broad, firm sands. Finally, you head back over the dunes of the Raven Meols Hills to the start. The combination of woods, dunes and beach is most attractive and the contrasting and extensive views take in the skyline of Liverpool and the hills of North Wales.

The dunes, woods, meadows and marshy slacks around Formby Point are the home of several rare creatures, including the red squirrel and natterjack toad. Much of the area comprises nature reserves and the whole of the coastline between Southport and Liverpool is one of the most extensive areas of sand dune in the country.

Start in front of the information

Formby Point

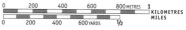

board and, with your back to it, walk along the tarmac drive ahead which bends right to exit from the car park. Turn left along Lifeboat Road and, at a T-junction, turn right Ⓐ along a broad, tree-lined track, part of the Sefton Coastal Footpath. Keep in more or less a straight line for the next ¾ mile (1.2km) – along first a tarmac track, then a rough track and finally sandy and grassy paths – to a crossroads. Continue ahead along a fence-lined path by the edge of the Cabin Hill Nature Reserve and, in front of the Altcar Rifle Ranges, follow the path to the right Ⓑ in the beach direction.

Head over the dunes to the beach. Ahead, the hills of North Wales are on the horizon and, to the left, the Wirral and the buildings of Liverpool can be seen. Turn right Ⓒ along the wide, sandy beach as far as the marker post 'Car Park, Information'. Just before reaching it, you pass the foundations of what is said to be the earliest lifeboat station in Britain. After becoming redundant, it served for a while as a tearoom.

At the marker post, turn right Ⓓ onto a path which heads over the dunes again, passing an observation platform – a superb viewpoint – before returning to the start.   ●

Foulridge – Reservoir and Canal

Start	Foulridge Wharf, signposted from A56 at Foulridge to the north of Colne
Distance	4 miles (6.4km)
Approximate time	2 hours
Parking	Foulridge Wharf
Refreshments	Pubs at Foulridge, tearoom at Foulridge Wharf
Ordnance Survey maps	Landranger 103 (Blackburn & Burnley), Explorers 21 (South Pennines) or 41 (Forest of Bowland & Ribblesdale)

The opening part of this route is beside Foulridge Lower Reservoir; the last stretch is along the towpath of the Leeds and Liverpool Canal. In between there is attractive and easy walking along enclosed, tree-lined tracks and field paths, with impressive views over the surrounding countryside.

The former textile village of Foulridge has an attractive green surrounded by old weavers' cottages. There are several reservoirs nearby and beyond the wharf, the Leeds and Liverpool Canal passes through a 1 mile (1.6km) long tunnel.

Facing the canal, turn left, not along the towpath which only leads to the tunnel entrance, but along the lane, heading gently uphill. Keep ahead past the Hole in the Wall pub and, at a T-junction, turn right into Sycamore Rise **A**. Follow the road around a left bend and, where it ends, keep ahead along an enclosed path which heads up to a road. Cross over and take the enclosed path opposite. This descends to the banks of Foulridge Lower Reservoir **B**.

Turn right onto a path that winds around the edge of the reservoir and then bears right by an outlet stream down to a lane **C**. Turn left and almost immediately right, at a public footpath

sign, along a tarmac track signposted to Holly Bush, Ball House, Sand Hall and Mistrals. At a fork, take the left-hand rough track, passing to the right of Sand Hall Farm, and, in front of a gate, turn right along an enclosed, tree- and hedge-lined path **D**. Here the route joins the Pendle Way, waymarked with Pendle Witch signs. The path heads gently uphill and where it bears left at the top, bear right to climb a stone stile. Walk along the right edge of a field, climb a stile onto a tarmac drive, climb the stile opposite and turn left along a track to another stile. After climbing that one, turn right and walk across a field to the next Pendle Way sign where you go through a wall gap and descend steps to a road. Turn right and, where the road bends right, turn sharp left **E** along a track, passing through a farm.

At a fork, take the left track, passing in front of bungalows, and, where it ends, go through a gate and along an

Foulridge Wharf

the left. Continue between farms and follow the track around a left bend, still keeping by the stream. At a fork, take the left-hand tarmac track which curves right and passes to the right of a former mill. Look out for where you go through a metal gate and keep ahead towards a bridge over the Leeds and Liverpool Canal. Climb a stile, cross the bridge and turn sharp right down steps to the towpath **F**. Turn left along it to return to Foulridge Wharf. ●

enclosed path. Climb a stone stile, keep along the left edge of a field, go through a gate and along an enclosed path to the right of a cottage. Descend steps to a tarmac track and turn right downhill, beside a rushing stream on

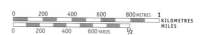

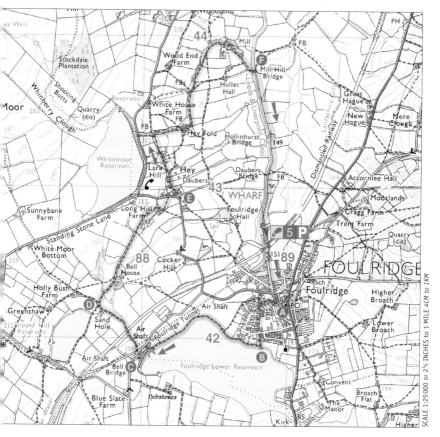

SCALE 1:25 000 or 2½ INCHES to 1 MILE 4CM to 1KM

Worsley and the Bridgewater Canal

Start	Worsley, Barton Road car park
Distance	5 miles (8km)
Approximate time	2½ hours
Parking	Worsley
Refreshments	Pubs at Worsley
Ordnance Survey maps	Landranger 109 (Manchester, Bolton & Warrington), Explorer 277 (Manchester & Salford)

Although it is difficult to escape from the noise of traffic on the M62 and other main roads, this is a most attractive walk, much of it through woodland. It also has considerable historic appeal as the section of the Bridgewater Canal between Worsley and Manchester was the pioneer canal of the Industrial Revolution and Worsley has many fine buildings from the canal era. The route makes use both of the canal towpath and the track of a disused railway.

Worsley can claim to be one of the birthplaces of the Industrial Revolution. In 1759 James Brindley began the construction of a canal to link the Duke of Bridgewater's coal mines at Worsley to Manchester. It was immediately successful – the price of coal in Manchester was halved – and sparked off the great canal boom of the second half of the 18th century during which canals were built all over the country. Several attractive, black and white buildings remain from the canal age. Foremost of these are the Packet House, originally built in 1760 – although the black-and-white timbering was added in the 19th century – and the Court House (opposite the car park), built in 1849.

Turn left out of the car park, passing the Court House, keep ahead at a roundabout to pass under the M62 and head uphill to Worsley's 19th-century church. At a roundabout by the church, bear left along Leigh Road, signposted to Boothstown, and after just over ¼ mile (400m), turn right, at a public footpath sign, along a tarmac track **Ⓐ**. At a fork, take the left hand track to continue across a golf course. Keep to the left of the hotel complex of Worsley Old Hall and, at a

Worsley

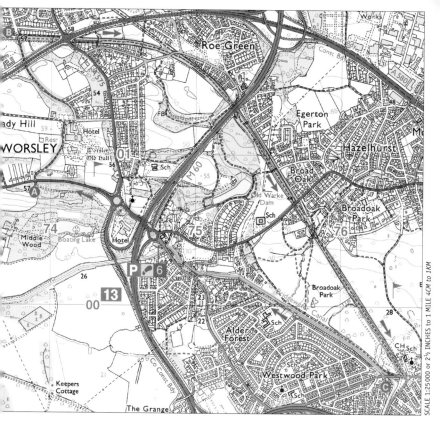

SCALE 1:25000 or 2½ INCHES to 1 MILE 4CM to 1KM

public footpath sign, turn right onto a tarmac path which descends to a drive.

Cross over, continue along the road ahead (Leigh Avenue) and where it ends, keep ahead along a path by a narrow belt of woodland on the left. Cross a busy dual carriageway, go through the gate opposite and continue along an enclosed path. Immediately after crossing a disused railway bridge, turn right **B**, at public footpath and Loopline signs, onto a path to the right of a house and continue along the left edge of woodland, beside garden fences on the left. Just before reaching a road, turn right down steps beside a bridge and turn left under the bridge to join the track of the disused Wigan to Eccles railway. Follow this track for just over 2 miles (3.2km) to Monton Green. At first the route is through a wooded cutting, then it passes Roe Green Junction (where the Bolton to Worsley

line joined the Wigan to Eccles line). After passing under the motorway and going past the site of Worsley station, the track runs along the top of an embankment. Here there are attractive views through the trees, both to the right and left.

Eventually, the track descends to a road at Monton Green. Turn right, cross a canal bridge, turn right onto the towpath of the Bridgewater Canal **C** and follow it back to Worsley. Approaching Worsley, go through a kissing gate, keep ahead to pass under an iron footbridge and, at the canal junction in front of the Packet House, turn left under Worsley Bridge. Turn left immediately up steps to the road and turn left over the bridge to return to the start. ●

Silverdale and Arnside Tower

Start	Silverdale, The Shore car park
Distance	4½ miles (7.2km)
Approximate time	2 hours
Parking	Silverdale
Refreshments	Pubs at Silverdale, tearoom at Witherslack Garden Centre
Ordnance Survey maps	Landranger 97 (Kendal & Morecambe), Outdoor Leisure 7 (The English Lakes – South Eastern area)

The opening and finishing stretches are along the grassy foreshore of Morecambe Bay. Apart from that, much of this attractive walk is through the beautiful limestone woodlands fringing the bay on the Lancashire-Cumbria border and the northern part of the route crosses into Cumbria to Arnside Tower. It is an easy walk, well-waymarked throughout, and there are fine views across the vast expanses of Morecambe Bay.

Begin by walking northwards along the shore, with the sea on the left, and, at a gap in the cliffs, turn right to a gate. Go through and keep ahead gently uphill along a tarmac track. To the right the houses of Silverdale and the tower of its 19th-century church can be seen.

Turn right at a T-junction Ⓐ along a lane, bear left onto a path which rises above it and, at a public footpath sign to Elmslack, the path curves left. The route continues in a straight line via a mixture of enclosed paths, tarmac drives and tracks to reach a T-junction. Turn left and, at a public footpath sign to Eaves Wood and Waterslack, immediately turn right onto a path which keeps close to the right edge of Eaves Wood.

At a wall corner keep ahead through the trees, heading downhill, turn left at a T-junction and follow the winding path to a fork.

Take the right-hand stony path gently downhill and squeeze through a wall gap onto a track by the entrance to Waterslack Garden Centre. Turn left towards the centre, go through the gate

Silverdale

to Orchard Cottage and continue along an enclosed track to a kissing gate. Go through, cross the railway line, go through another kissing gate and turn left along a lane **B**. Soon, Arnside Knott comes into view. At a public footpath sign to Arnside Tower, follow the lane around a left bend towards a quarry, recross the railway line and, in front of the quarry entrance, turn right along a path through trees **C**.

At a fork take the left-hand path, signposted to Arnside Tower and Knott, which curves left and continues close to the right edge of Middlebarrow Wood, below Arnside Knott. Go through a gate on the far edge of the wood and head uphill to the ruined Arnside Tower **D**, one of a chain of peel towers built around Morecambe Bay in the 14th century to protect the area from Scottish coastal raids. Part of it blew down in a great gale in 1602.

Pass to the left of the tower, keep ahead between redundant gateposts and walk along an enclosed path, signposted 'Silverdale via Cove Road'. Go through a gate and continue along the hedge-lined path to emerge into a caravan site. Bear left, cross a tarmac drive and continue along a parallel drive. To the right are views over Morecambe Bay.

Cross another drive to a footpath sign and follow its direction across grass, through a gap in a belt of trees and along the right edge of a field to go through a gate onto a lane. Turn left and, where the lane bends left, turn right **A** along a tarmac track, at a sign 'The Shore'. Rejoin the outward route and retrace your steps to the start. ●

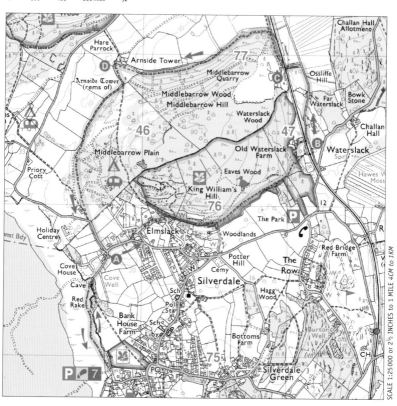

Poulton-Le-Fylde and Skippool Creek

Start	Poulton-le-Fylde
Distance	5 miles (8km)
Approximate time	2½ hours
Parking	Reach, car park in corner of village green
Refreshments	Pubs and cafés at Poulton-le-Fylde, pubs at Skippool
Ordnance Survey maps	Landranger 102 (Preston & Blackpool), Explorers 286 (Blackpool & Preston) and 296 (Lancaster, Morecambe & Fleetwood)

A short walk across fields from Poulton-le-Fylde brings you to Skippool Creek, formerly a busy port and a centre for smuggling activities. The route then continues beside the creek and then alongside the Wyre estuary before turning away from the river to return to the start. There are grand views across the estuary and over the flat expanses of the Fylde, with the familiar landmark of Blackpool Tower visible at times.

The walk begins in the Market Square which is overlooked by Poulton's fine 18th-century church. The west tower is earlier, built in the 1630s. Walk along the pedestrianised Church Street, passing to the left of the church, to a T-junction and turn right. Keep ahead at a crossroads along Vicarage Road, turn left at a T-junction to cross a railway bridge and immediately turn right onto an enclosed, tarmac path, at a public footpath sign to Moorland Road.

The path emerges onto a road (Haworth Crescent). Continue along it and, where it ends, bear left along an enclosed, tarmac path – between a school on the right and a playing field on the left – to a road. Turn right and, where the main road bends right, turn left **A**, along Little Poulton Lane, an attractive mixture of old cottages and modern houses. The lane curves left and, where it ends, keep ahead along a track to a stile. Climb it, continue along a hedge-lined path to emerge into a field and turn right along its right edge. Follow the edge to the left to continue above Main Dyke, climb a stile and keep ahead along an enclosed path which follows the meanderings of the dyke to a road **B**. Cross over, turn left and, at a roundabout – just before reaching a road on the right – turn right over a stile to join the Wyre Way **C**.

Turn left and the path bends right alongside Skippool Creek to a lane. Skippool was once a busy port on the River Wyre and a notorious centre for smuggling activities. It declined after 1840 because of competition from nearby Fleetwood and the development of larger vessels.

Bear right to continue first beside the

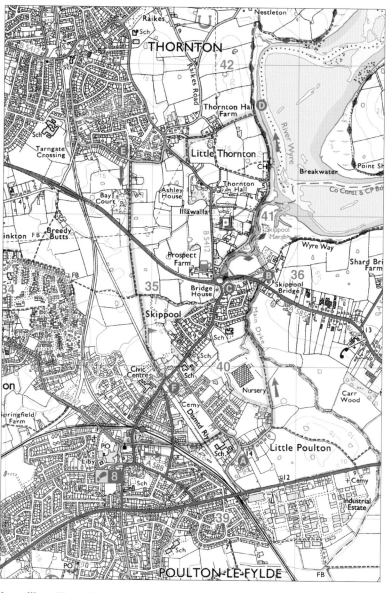

creek and then by the Wyre estuary to a fingerpost. The route continues along a track beside the estuary, in the 'Stanah via Ramper Pot' direction, below a wooded embankment. At the next fingerpost, turn left **D**, over a stile at a gap in the embankment, following the sign to Little Thornton, climb steps and walk along the left edge of a field towards a farm. Climb a stile, keep ahead to climb another stile and continue along a track, passing in front of Thornton Hall Farm. Blackpool Tower can be seen at this point. At a public footpath sign, turn left up steps, climb a stile and walk along the left edge of a field. Climb a stile at a fence corner to the right of a hut, keep ahead to a road and turn right.

At a T-junction by a small triangular green, turn left along Tarn Road, follow it around a right bend and at a public footpath sign to Poulton-le-Fylde, turn left along a straight, fence-lined, tarmac track 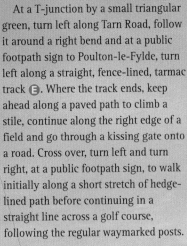. Where the track ends, keep ahead along a paved path to climb a stile, continue along the right edge of a field and go through a kissing gate onto a road. Cross over, turn left and turn right, at a public footpath sign, to walk initially along a short stretch of hedge-lined path before continuing in a straight line across a golf course, following the regular waymarked posts.

At a crossroads by a fingerpost, keep ahead, in the Poulton direction, by a ditch on the right and, after crossing a footbridge, turn right to a footpath post and then turn left to continue along the right edge of the golf course.

In the corner, climb a stile and keep ahead along a narrow, enclosed path to emerge onto a road ⑥. Turn right, keep ahead at a crossroads, continue past the station and turn right at a crossroads beside the church. Turn left into Church Street to return to the Market Square. ●

Skippool Creek

Slaidburn and Newton

Start	Slaidburn
Distance	5 miles (8km)
Approximate time	2½ hours
Parking	Slaidburn
Refreshments	Pub and café at Slaidburn, pub at Newton
Ordnance Survey maps	Landranger 103 (Blackburn & Burnley), Outdoor Leisure 41 (Forest of Bowland & Ribblesdale)

Although a relatively short and undemanding route, there are superb views over the Bowland fells and Hodder valley, two attractive and interesting villages and pleasant moorland, woodland and riverside walking. The final stretch is a delightful and relaxing ramble beside the River Hodder.

A street of attractive stone cottages leads up from the old bridge over the River Hodder to the village centre and the Hark to Bounty Inn. Slaidburn used to be the administrative centre of the Forest of Bowland and the forest courts met in what is now the inn, where the courtroom is still preserved. The mainly 15th-century church is on the edge of the village, seen near the end of the walk.

The walk begins at the car park by the bridge over the River Hodder. Turn right to walk up through the

Slaidburn Bridge

village, keep ahead past the Hark to Bounty and just after passing Slaidburn Health Centre, bear right through a fence gap  **A** onto a path which heads downhill through trees to Croasdale Brook. The path continues beside the brook to a ladder stile. Climb it, keep ahead to emerge from the trees and head up away from the brook to climb another stile. Keep ahead along the right edge of a field and, just before reaching a ladder stile in the field corner, turn sharp left and head diagonally uphill to climb a stile onto a lane **B**.

Cross over and take the moorland track ahead to Pain Hill Farm. As it winds across the moorland, there are grand and imposing views to the right of the Bowland fells. Go through a gate into the farmyard, turn right in front of the house, go through another gate and turn left at the corner of a barn to continue along a track beside a wall on the left. After climbing a stone stile to the left of a gate, follow the track as it bears slightly left across the field corner to join a wall and keep beside it towards the next farm. Climb a stone stile to the left of a gate, head across a field to climb a ladder stile in the corner, then bear right and head across the next field, passing to the left of the farm buildings.

Climb two stiles in quick succession and walk across the next field, making for a stone stile. After climbing this, keep along the right edge of a field. On approaching a farm, bear left away from the field edge, keep to the left of the farm, climb a stile and cross a plank footbridge. Keep ahead to climb another stile onto a lane **C**. Turn left and follow the narrow lane downhill into Newton, passing a Quaker burial ground and former meeting house, both dating from the 18th century. Persecution of the Quakers at the time caused them to seek out small and relatively isolated places like Newton.

At a T-junction, turn left through the village and, at a fork, take the right-hand road, signposted to Waddington and Clitheroe. Turn right at a T-junction, follow the road down to the bridge over the River Hodder, passing the Parkers Arms, and at a public footpath sign in front of the bridge **D**, turn left through a gate. Walk along the right edge of a field, go through another gate, descend some steps and continue along a rocky and uneven path beside the Hodder. Cross a footbridge over a tributary brook and keep ahead along the right edge of a field.

Look out for where you turn right over another footbridge and climb a stone stile. Turn left along the left edge of a meadow and, at the far tapering end, climb a stile and continue above the river along the bottom inside edge of Great Dunnow Wood. After going through a kissing gate, keep ahead across a meadow to a track, turn left and follow it below steep, wooded slopes to a 'Riverside Path' footpath post. Ahead is a fine view of Slaidburn Church.

Walk past the footpath post to go through a gate and immediately turn right over a stile **E**, also signed 'Riverside Path'. A path – a permissive route – leads to a stile. Climb it, keep ahead through trees to climb another one and turn left to follow a path beside the Hodder, over stiles and through a kissing gate, back to the start. ●

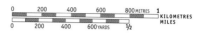

Barrowford and Roughlee

Start	Barrowford, Pendle Heritage Centre
Distance	4 miles (6.4km)
Approximate time	2 hours
Parking	Pendle Heritage Centre
Refreshments	Pubs at Barrowford, café at Pendle Heritage Centre, pub at Roughlee
Ordnance Survey maps	Landranger 103 (Blackburn & Burnley), Outdoor Leisure 41 (Forest of Bowland & Ribblesdale) or 21 (South Pennines)

Much of the first part of the route is through the valley of Pendle Water. A brief climb out of the valley is followed by a descent into Roughlee, a village which has associations with the Pendle Witches. After crossing stepping stones, the return to Barrowford is mainly along tracks and field paths, with a final section through Barrowford Park. The many fine views are dominated by Pendle Hill and Blacko Tower and extend to the edge of the Brontë moors.

The Pendle Heritage Centre, on the opposite side of the road from the car park, is housed in a 16th-century manor house and comprises a museum, shop, cafe and tourist information centre. There is also a cruck barn and walled garden.

Go through a gate in the car park, at a Pendle Way sign, and walk along a path beside Pendle Water on the left to emerge onto a road at the side of Higherford Old Bridge. Turn left over the bridge and turn right **A** along a lane called Foreside - now with Pendle Water on the right - passing an old pack-horse bridge. The route continues along an attractive, tree-lined path beside the stream, going through two gates, to reach a T-junction. Turn right over a bridge and turn left over a stile to walk along the other bank.

Turn left to cross a tributary stream (Blacko Water) at the next footbridge, turn right and head uphill across a field, bearing slightly left away from the stream, to a stile. Climb it, keep ahead

Roughlee Hall

to climb another one and walk along the right edge of a field. Climb a stile, keep ahead along the right field edge, climb another stile to the left of a farm, walk along an enclosed path and go through a gate onto a road 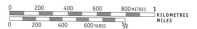 **B**.

Cross over, take the uphill track ahead to Bank End Farm and climb a stile to the left of a cattle grid. Continue uphill across a field, veering left away from the field edge. Climb a stile, cross a track and continue walking up to climb a stone stile. Turn left along a path through conifers, which passes to the right of the farm, and then climb a stone stile into woodland. Bear left and head downhill through this beautiful woodland, looking out for where you climb another stone stile at its bottom edge.

Walk along the right edge of a field,

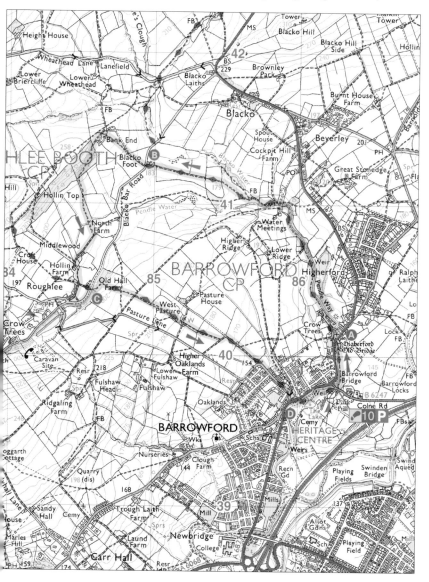

Pendle Water

turn right over a stone stile just before reaching the corner and turn left along a left field edge, veering away from it to go through a gate. Keep ahead across the next field and, on the far side, turn right to continue along its left edge to a gate. Go through, walk along a tarmac drive, passing to the right of a cottage, go through another gate and turn left between farm buildings.

Head gently downhill along a tarmac track and, at a fork, take the right hand track to pass in front of Roughlee Old Hall. This fine 17th-century building, now divided into a number of separate cottages, was the alleged home of Alice Nutter, one of the Pendle Witches, hanged at Lancaster Castle in 1612. Where the track ends, continue along an enclosed path in front of cottages which bears left to reach the road in Roughlee. Turn left and, at a Pendle Way sign, turn right over a stile Ⓒ, descend a bank and cross stepping stones over Pendle Water.

Head up the bank on the other side,

making for a footpath post, and bear right across a field and over a brow to a stile. Climb it, walk along the right edge of the next two fields, heading steadily downhill, and go through a gate in the bottom corner of the second field. Turn left over a stile, pass to the left of a barn, climb another stile and keep ahead along a hedge-lined path which continues along the left edge of a field. In the bottom corner of the field, cross a footbridge, turn left along a fence-lined path, climb a stile and turn right along a tarmac track.

Head downhill along the track to a road by Pasture Gate House and turn left steeply downhill into Barrowford, bending right to a T-junction. Cross the footbridge almost opposite into Barrowford Park Ⓓ and turn left onto a tarmac path beside Pendle Water again. The park was laid out for local people in the 1920s by two cotton manufacturers. The path leads back to the Pendle Heritage Centre and the start of the route.

Whalley, River Calder and Read Park

Start	Spring Wood Picnic Site, at junction of A671 and B6246 $^1/_2$ mile (800m) to the east of Whalley
Distance	5$^1/_2$ miles (8.9km)
Approximate time	3 hours
Parking	Spring Wood Picnic Site
Refreshments	Pubs and cafés at Whalley, coffee shop at Whalley Abbey, pub near Cock Bridge
Ordnance Survey maps	Landranger 103 (Blackburn & Burnley), Explorer 287 (West Pennine Moors)

A brief descent into Whalley is followed by a climb over the wooded slopes of Whalley Nab and a lovely stretch above or beside the River Calder. After a pleasant stroll through Read Park, there are superb views over Whalley and the Calder and Ribble valleys on the final descent. Historic interest is provided by the ancient crosses, medieval church and abbey ruins at Whalley, two Victorian railway viaducts and Read Hall. None of the climbing is particularly steep or strenuous.

Start by leaving the picnic site and crossing the road – just to the right of the traffic lights – to a public footpath sign and take a path which bears right through trees to a stile. Climb it, head diagonally downhill across a field, making for the trees on its right side, and climb a stile in the bottom right-hand corner. Bear left along a track, go through a gate, bear left along a tarmac track to emerge onto a road in Whalley and turn left **A** through the village.

Whalley has an interesting religious heritage. The fine medieval church dates mainly from the 13th century and in the churchyard are three rare Dark Age crosses. Nearby, are the ruins of a Cistercian abbey, founded in 1283. All that survives of the church are the

foundations, but there are two well-preserved gatehouses and substantial remains of some of the domestic buildings. The last abbot of Whalley was hanged in 1537 for taking part in the Pilgrimage of Grace, a rebellion against Henry VIII's closure of the monasteries, and the Elizabethan house on the site was built by the Assheton family after the dissolution. Just beyond the 14th-century north-west gateway are the great redbrick arches of the Victorian viaduct which carries the railway high above the Calder valley.

Keep ahead to cross the bridge over the River Calder and immediately turn left along a narrow lane (Moor Lane) which heads steeply uphill. Where the lane curves right, turn left **B**, at a public bridleway sign, along a path

River Calder near Whalley

which continues uphill through trees over Whalley Nab. At a bench, there is a choice between continuing along the bridleway or the parallel footpath – the footpath is best for the superb views over Whalley and the Calder valley.

After the reunion of the footpath and bridleway, continue steeply uphill over the Nab to reach a track and bear left along it, passing to the right of a house. Go through a gate, keep ahead along an enclosed path to a lane and continue along it between cottages to where it bends right. Keep ahead, at a public footpath sign to Great Harwood, along a track and, at a footpath sign, bear left to continue along the bridleway, not the parallel footpath to the left.

Follow this sunken, enclosed path downhill and, just in front of a barn, turn left over a stile Ⓒ. Head downhill across a field to a stile in the bottom corner, climb it and walk along the left edge of a field, by a brook on the left. Climb another stile, ford the brook, keep ahead – now with the brook on the right – recross it by a footbridge and continue downhill across the next field,

descending steeply to cross a footbridge over a brook to the right of its confluence with the River Calder.

Keep ahead over a ladder stile, climb a flight of steps through trees and continue high above the river to a kissing gate. Go through, bear left to continue above the Calder – there are superb views to the left of the bends in the river – and the path descends quite steeply to ford a brook. Keep ahead by the river and, after crossing a footbridge over another tributary brook, bear right uphill and climb a stile onto the A680, just below the Game Cock Inn.

Turn left downhill to cross Cock Bridge and, at a public footpath sign, turn right Ⓓ along the tarmac drive to Read Garden Centre. Continue along the uphill enclosed track to the left of the garden centre entrance, by the edge of Cock Wood. To the right, there are views of the now disused 19th-century Martholme Viaduct. The track emerges via a gate onto the A671 Ⓔ. Cross over, go through gates and past a lodge and walk along the tarmac track through Read Park. Occasional glimpses of Read

Hall, built in the early 19th century, can be seen through the trees ahead.

At a fork, take the left-hand track and, just before entering woodland, turn left over a stile. Walk along the right edge of a series of fields, via gates and stiles, and the track eventually emerges through a kissing gate onto a lane by Read Old Bridge **F**. Turn left over the bridge, follow the lane uphill to a junction and keep ahead, in the Whalley direction, to a T-junction. Turn right along a lane (Clerk Hill Road) and, at a public footpath sign, turn left over a stone stile **G**. Walk across a field, climb a stile on the far side, bear right and head uphill over a brow, making for a waymarked stile ahead. From here there are grand views over Whalley and the Calder and Ribble valleys, with the Victorian railway viaduct prominent.

About 100 yds (91m) before reaching the stile, turn left and head downhill across the field, making for the left corner of Spring Wood where you bear left to cross a footbridge. Bear right to continue along the right edge of Whalley golf course and, just before reaching the road, a stile on the right leads back to the start.

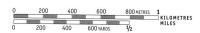

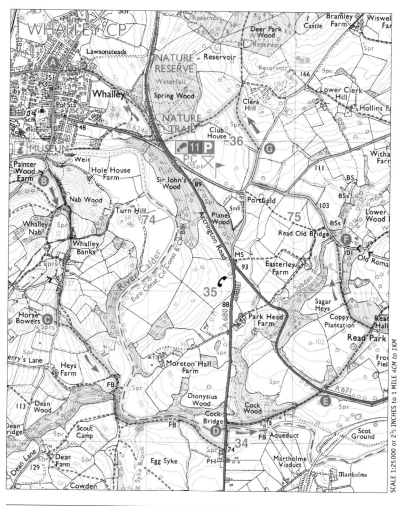

Darwen Moor

Start	Roddlesworth Information Centre, about 1 mile (1.6km) south of Tockholes
Distance	4 miles (6.4km)
Approximate time	2 hours
Parking	Roddlesworth
Refreshments	Pub at start, pub by Sunnyhurst Wood
Ordnance Survey maps	Landranger 103 (Blackburn & Burnley), Explorer 287 (West Pennine Moors)

Darwen Moor is one of the larger expanses of heather moorland on the West Pennine Moors and access to it was only won in 1896 after an 18-year legal battle waged by local people. Most of the walk is on well-defined moorland tracks and for much of the way Darwen Tower is in sight. From the tower, 1220 ft (372m) high, you enjoy contrasting views of industrial and rural Lancashire. All the gradients are easy and gradual.

Turn left out of the car park and, almost immediately, turn left again, at a public bridleway sign, into Hollinshead Terrace. Turn right, by the end of the terrace, along a track to a gate. Go through the gate onto the open moorland and walk along a gently ascending track. The first part of the route, up to the tower, is indicated by a series of marker stones with the distinctive outline of Darwen Tower carved on them.

Go through a gate at the corner of a wood, keep ahead through the narrow belt of trees and go through another gate at the far end where the main track does a U-bend to the left. Continue steadily uphill, later by a tumbling beck on the right, go through a gate **A** and keep ahead along a path which winds across the open moorland, curving left to reach another gate.

Go through and, at the fork immediately in front, take the left-hand path. At the next fork, take the left-hand path again to continue across the top of the moor. The path later curves right and continues to another fork. Take the right-hand upper path which leads to

Darwen Moor

Darwen Tower, reached by a brief detour to the right **B**. The tower was erected in 1897 to commemorate Queen Victoria's Diamond Jubilee and the sweeping and contrasting views include the mills and terraces of Blackburn and Darwen, dominated by the tall chimney of India Mill, the West Pennine Moors, Forest of Bowland and the Fylde.

Return to the main path, continue along it and at a fork, take the left-hand path which descends, curves left and heads quite steeply down to a gate. Go through, continue downhill and take the left-hand path at a fork which descends between wooded banks to emerge onto a road in front of the Sunnyhurst pub Turn left **C** and after passing to the left of the Sunnyhurst Wood car park, the way continues along an enclosed track.

At a fork by a large stone-built house, take the left-hand track which heads gently uphill between reservoirs – Sunnyhurst Hey above on the left and Earnsdale below on the right. After about $\frac{1}{4}$ mile (400m), look out for where a grassy track leads off to the right **D** and heads down towards trees to a stile. Climb it, continue downhill across a field, climb another stile and keep ahead across the next field, making for the left edge of trees.

The path curves right to a gate. Go through, head uphill along the left field edge to climb a stile and continue to a gate in the field corner. Go through, turn left along a track and, at a fork immediately ahead, take the right-hand, tree-lined track to emerge onto a road. Turn left to the start. ●

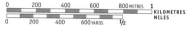

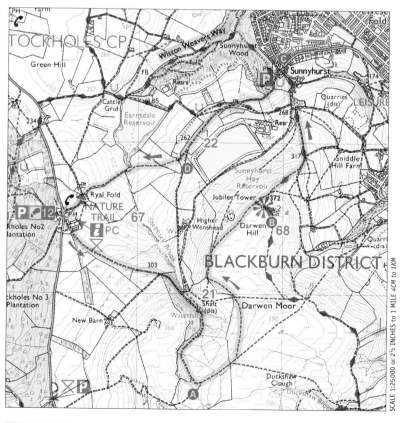

Pilling

Start	Pilling, car park
Distance	5½ miles (8.9km)
Approximate time	2½ hours
Parking	Pilling
Refreshments	Café at Pilling
Ordnance Survey maps	Landranger 102 (Preston & Blackpool), Explorer 296 (Lancaster, Morecambe & Fleetwood)

The highlight of this invigorating walk on the Fylde coast is the stretch of just over 1 mile (1.6km) along the sea wall above the mudflats and marshes of Morecambe Bay. There are extensive views both across the bay and over the Fylde, and the tower and spire of Pilling Church is in sight for much of the way. Some of the field paths on the initial inland part of the walk may be muddy at times.

Turn left out of the car park, follow the road round to the right, ignore a public footpath sign on the right but about 100 yds (91m) beyond it, turn right through a gate **A**. Walk along an enclosed track between houses, go through another gate, bear left and head diagonally across a field to cross a footbridge in the corner.

Turn left along the left edge of fields to emerge onto a lane. Take the enclosed track ahead and, where it bends right, keep ahead along a hedge-lined path to a stile. After climbing it, continue along the left edge of a succession of fields, climbing a series of stiles and crossing a footbridge. In the corner of the final field, cross a footbridge over a drain, turn right and go through a waymarked gate onto a track. Turn left to a lane **B**, keep ahead, follow the lane around a right bend and, at a public footpath sign, turn left along a tarmac track **C**. Where the track bends left, turn right **D**, at a

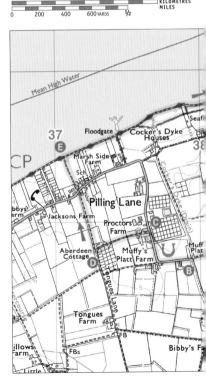

public footpath sign, along a path that keeps beside the right bank of a drain, climbing two stiles and finally going through a kissing gate onto a road. Cross over, climb the stone stile opposite and continue by the left bank of the drain, climbing more stiles to reach an embankment. Climb it and turn right **E** to follow a tarmac path along the top of the embankment above the shore. The views are immense: to the right, across the Fylde, to the left, across Morecambe Bay to Heysham Power Station and the Lake District mountains on the horizon, and ahead to Lancaster and the Bowland fells.

The path eventually descends to a lane by a car park **F**. Follow the lane back to Pilling and, at a T-junction, turn right and walk through the village, passing to the left of the 19th-century church, to the car park. ●

Pilling church

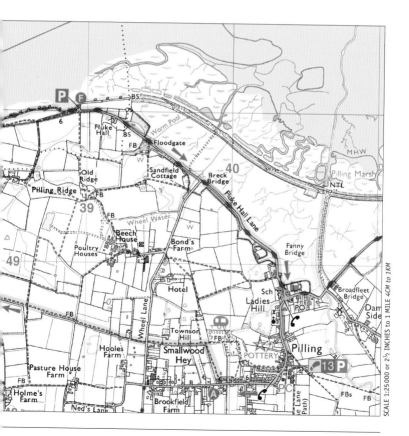

SCALE 1:25000 or 2½ INCHES to 1 MILE 4CM to 1KM

Lune Valley – Kirkby Lonsdale to Whittington

Start	Kirkby Lonsdale, Devil's Bridge
Distance	6 ¼ miles (10.1km) Shorter version 5 miles (8km)
Approximate time	3 hours (2½ hours for shorter walk)
Parking	Devil's Bridge, parking areas on both sides of the bridge
Refreshments	Kiosk at Devil's Bridge, pubs and cafés at Kirkby Lonsdale, pub at Whittington
Ordnance Survey maps	Landranger 97 (Kendal & Morecambe), Outdoor Leisure 2 (Yorkshire Dales – Southern and Western areas)

Most of the route is a 'there and back' riverside walk, following the Lune Valley Ramble along an outstandingly attractive stretch of the Lune. Loops at each end enable you first to walk through the delightful town of Kirkby Lonsdale – just across the Cumbrian border – to see the Norman church and Ruskin's View, and second to divert across fields to the village of Whittington. The shorter version omits Kirkby Lonsdale. The superb riverside views include the distinctive landmark of Ingleborough.

Devil's Bridge is a most attractive and deservedly popular spot. The bridge – a handsome structure – spans the steep, wooded, rocky banks of the Lune and there are fine views both upstream and downstream. The walk begins on its west side.

🖉 If doing the shorter walk, go through a squeezer stile and down steps, at a public footpath sign to Whittington, and pick up the route directions from where the full walk returns to the start.

For the full route, walk along the lane away from the bridge and, at a public footpath sign to Town, turn right along an enclosed tarmac path. Head gently uphill, go under a bridge and, at a fork, take the left-hand path into Kirkby Lonsdale's Market Square. Turn right

along Main Street, turn left at a T-junction, turn right along Church Street, beside the Sun Hotel, and go through gates into the churchyard. The 12th-century church has a fine Norman west door at the base of the tower and retains some of the original Norman aisles in the nave. It also has a superb 13th-century lancet window at the east end.

Pass to the left of the church and bear right to a footpath post. A brief detour to the left along a terrace brings you to Ruskin's View, a magnificent viewpoint overlooking a great bend in the River Lune and the fells beyond. Turner painted this scene in 1822 which Ruskin was later to describe as 'One of the loveliest in England, therefore in the world'.

At the footpath post descend a long flight of steps – the Radical Steps – and, at the bottom, turn right **Ⓐ** onto a riverside path. Keep by the wooded riverbank, following the Lune around a right bend and through two kissing gates, to emerge onto the lane at the start by Devil's Bridge.

Cross over, go through a squeezer stile and down steps opposite, at a public footpath sign to Whittington, and walk across a picnic area towards the road bridge which carries the A65

Lune valley near Whittington

by the right edge of the hedge down to a pair of gates where you meet the previous track. Go through the gate in front and continue along the left edge of a succession of fields and through a series of gates to reach a road **C**.

Turn left into Whittington and, where the road bends left, turn right along Church Street. At a public footpath sign, turn left through gates and up steps into the churchyard and pass to the right of the church. From here there is a fine view over the Lune valley. The 15th-century tower is the oldest part of the church; the rest was mainly rebuilt in 1875. Descend steps to go through a squeezer stile and bear left along the left edge of a churchyard extension to a gate. Go through, walk along the left edge of a field, go through a kissing gate and continue along the right edge of the next field to a squeezer stile in the corner. After going through, keep ahead along an enclosed tarmac path to rejoin the main road through the village.

Turn right and, where the road bends right, turn left **D**, at a public bridleway sign, along an enclosed track. Follow it around several bends to a gate, go through and the track curves left to reach the Lune again **E**. Keep beside the river to a stile, climb it and continue across a meadow to climb another stile at the far tapering end. Walk along the right edge of the next meadow and, after climbing a stile **B**, you rejoin the outward route and retrace your steps to Devil's Bridge. ●

over the river. Go through a kissing gate in front of the bridge, turn right up to the road, cross over, turn left down to another kissing gate, go through and turn right. The way now continues for nearly 1¼ miles (2km) across meadows beside the Lune, via a series of gates and stiles and with superb riverside views.

At a waymarked post – just after climbing a Lune Valley Ramble stile – which indicates a path to the right, turn right along the right edge of a field **B**. The tower of Whittington Church is seen ahead. Continue along an enclosed track, go through a gate and cross a footbridge over a beck. Although the track ahead is rejoined later, the right-of-way bears left off it, across grass, and heads gently uphill towards a low hill. Bear right to follow the base of the hill around to a hedge corner and keep

The Yealands and Leighton Hall

Start	Tewitfield Locks, signposted from A6 to the north of Carnforth
Distance	6½ miles (10.5km)
Approximate time	3 hours
Parking	Tewitfield Locks
Refreshments	Pub at start, pub at Yealand Conyers, tearoom at Leighton Hall
Ordnance Survey	Landranger 97 (Kendal & Morecambe), Outdoor Leisure 7 (The English Lakes – South Eastern area)

This is a superb walk which, for a modest effort, rewards you with a series of extensive and magnificent views which range across Morecambe Bay to the Furness peninsula, the peaks of southern Lakeland and the line of the Pennines. The only fairly steep climb is over the ridge between Leighton Hall and Yealand Conyers. It also provides plenty of variety: pleasant canalside walking at the start, attractive woodland, two villages and the opportunity to visit a stately home.

Begin by walking in front of the Longlands Hotel to a lane, turn left and then left again along the main road. Just before crossing the bridge over the M6, turn right down steps to the

Woodlands of White Moss

towpath of the Lancaster Canal and turn right along it. Despite the inevitable noise from the motorway, this is a pleasant stretch of the canal beside some of the disused Tewitfield Locks. There were eight of them and they raised the canal some 246 ft (75m) in ½ mile (800m). At a footbridge and a public footpath sign to Leighton Hall, turn sharp left **Ⓐ** through a gate and walk along an enclosed track which bends right to pass under the M6. Go through another gate, turn right and continue along the right edge of a field parallel to the motorway. In the corner, turn left

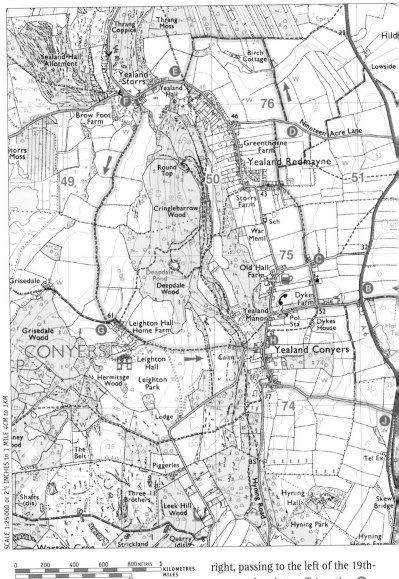

SCALE 1:25 000 or 2½ INCHES to 1 MILE 4CM to 1KM

0 200 400 600 800 METRES   1
| | | | | KILOMETRES
                              MILES
0 200 400 600 YARDS ½

to keep along the right field edge, go through a gate, turn right along the right edge of the next field and follow the edge as it curves left to another gate. Go through, keep ahead and, after the next gate, cross a railway bridge and continue along an enclosed track to the A6 **B**. Cross carefully, keep ahead along an uphill lane into Yealand Conyers and take the first lane on the

right, passing to the left of the 19th-century church, to a T-junction **C**.

The Yealands are two rather straggling adjacent villages – Yealand Conyers and Yealand Redmayne – that were originally one but became divided through inheritance by different families. Many of the farms and cottages date from the 17th and 18th centuries. In the 17th century, the villages became a stronghold of the Quaker religion and the tiny meeting house, passed near the end of the walk,

go through a gate to emerge onto the end of a road on the edge of Yealand Redmayne.

Immediately, turn right along an enclosed path, signposted to Nineteen Acre Lane, to a gate, go through and keep ahead along a fence-lined path to another gate. After going through that one, the route continues more or less in a straight line, mainly along the right edge of a succession of small fields and via a series of combinations of gates and stone stiles, to emerge onto a lane. Turn right and, after about 100 yds (91m), turn left along a straight, hedge-lined track **D**.

Ahead are the dense woodlands of White Moss, with the Lakeland fells on the horizon. At a T-junction turn left and continue along an enclosed path by the left edge of the woods to a gate. Go through, keep ahead along a beautiful tree-lined path and, where it bends right, turn left through a gate. Walk along the right edge of a field and, just before reaching the corner, bear left to a gate. After going through it, head gently uphill across a field, making for a gate in the far right corner. Go through, immediately turn left through another one onto a lane **E** and turn right.

Where the lane bends right, turn left over a stone stile **F**, at a public footpath sign to Leighton Hall, walk along a track and go through a gate. The way now continues along a grassy track across a series of fields – sometimes by the right edge and later by the left edge – and through a succession of gates, finally heading across the last field to go through a gate onto a tarmac track in front of a house **G**. On this stretch of the walk, there are fine views ahead over Morecambe Bay and to the right the woods, pools and wetlands of Leighton Moss Nature Reserve can be seen. Turn

was built in 1692. It is one of the oldest in the country.

At the T-junction turn left for the village pub but the route continues ahead along an enclosed path, signposted to Well Lane. After going through a gate, immediately turn right through another gate, turn left along the left edge of a field and climb a stone stile in the corner. Veer left across a field, climb a stone stile, continue diagonally across the next field and climb a stile onto a track. Turn left and

Leighton Hall

left gently uphill along the tarmac drive, passing to the left of Leighton Hall, and go through a gate beside a cattle grid. The entrance to the hall is to the right. Leighton Hall, originally a medieval manor house, was rebuilt in the Gothic style in the 18th century and refaced in pale grey limestone in the early 19th century. As the home of the Gillow family – Waring and Gillow were famous furniture manufacturers in Lancaster – it possesses some fine examples of Gillow furniture. There are attractive gardens and an unusual collection of birds of prey.

The route continues ahead steeply uphill across grass, initially following a line of telegraph posts. Later you keep to the right of a small plantation and continue up to a bench on the brow of the hill. Sit on it for a while to admire the magnificent view: Leighton Hall lies below and beyond that the nature reserve, the wooded coastline of Morecambe Bay, the long line of the Furness peninsula and the fells of southern Lakeland.

Keep ahead through trees and past a waymarked post to a kissing gate, go through and continue over the brow, passing a cairn. Now comes another superb view through the trees ahead of the Pennines, with Ingleborough standing out prominently. Descend steeply through the trees, climb a stone stile near the end of a wall, keep ahead past two waymarked posts and go through a gate onto a lane. Turn left downhill into Yealand Conyers to a T-junction 🄷.

The Quaker meeting house is to the left but the route continues to the right to another T-junction in front of the Catholic church. Turn left downhill along a lane to the A6 🄹, cross carefully and climb steps opposite, at a public footpath sign to Tewitfield. Cross the railway line very carefully – this is the main west coast route between London and Scotland – bear left to a kissing gate, go through and keep ahead along the right edge of a field.

Go through a gate in the corner, continue along an enclosed track and after going through a gate, turn right along a tarmac track which bends left to another gate by a cottage. Go through and the track bends right up to a road. Turn left and cross the bridge over the M6 to return to the start. ●

Parbold Hill and The Fairy Glen

Start	Parbold, by the Railway Station
Distance	6 miles (9.7km)
Approximate time	3 hours
Parking	Parbold, Station car park
Refreshments	Pubs and café at Parbold
Ordnance Survey maps	Landranger 108 (Liverpool, Southport & Wigan), Explorer 285 (Southport & Chorley)

Parbold Hill, one of the most westerly spurs of the Pennines and a superb viewpoint, rises to 420 ft (128m) above the West Lancashire plain. The ascent is through the delightful wooded ravine of the Fairy Glen and the descent is across fields. Both the ascent and descent are easy and gradual and the final stretch is a relaxing stroll along the towpath of the Leeds and Liverpool Canal.

Go over the level crossing and walk along Station Road, crossing the canal and keeping ahead to a T-junction. Turn left and, almost immediately, turn right along Bradshaw Lane **Ⓐ**. Where the lane bends right to a house, turn left over a stile and walk along the right edge of a field. Climb a stile, keep ahead by a brook on the left, cross a foot-bridge over the brook and climb the

Fairy Glen

stile ahead to a T-junction. Turn right, cross a footbridge over the River Douglas, bear left and head across a field to climb a stile in the far corner.

Walk along a track to Prior's Wood Farm, pass between the farm buildings, turning first left and then right, and continue along a track to a stile. Climb it, keep along a left field edge – later beside woodland on the left – go through a gate and continue to a T-junction **B**. Turn left, climb a stile, recross the River Douglas and keep ahead to cross the Leeds and Liverpool Canal. Continue along a track which winds steadily uphill between trees, cross a railway and keep ahead to a crossroads **C**.

Turn right, go through a gate, pass in front of a house and bear slightly right along a path to a stile. Climb it to enter woodland, continue along a broad track and, where it bends left, bear right over a stile. Head over a slight rise, continue across the field to climb a stile, keep ahead across the next field and, on the far side, do not climb the stile in front but turn left along the field edge to another stile about 50 yds (46m) ahead. This stile admits you to the wooded ravine of the Fairy Glen.

Descend steps, cross a footbridge over Sprodley Brook, climb steps on the other side and, at the top, turn left to continue along a path beside the brook. Turn left over a footbridge by a water-fall, turn right and climb steps to rejoin the brook. Do not cross the next foot-bridge but continue along the left side of the brook and, where the path curves right, turn sharp left over a stile. Climb more steps, and then a stile onto a track, turn right and follow the track to the main road at the top of Parbold Hill **D**.

Turn right and, at a layby, turn left over a stile and walk along the right edge of a field. Follow the field edge to the left, climb a stile, continue through

a belt of trees and the path later bears right and keeps along the left edge of Sprodley Brook. Climb two more stiles in quick succession and keep ahead – later by the right edge of a conifer plantation – to reach a field. Continue straight across it, passing to the left of some small tree-enclosed pools, and turn right along a grassy track. Continue to a T-junction and turn left **E** along a track, initially tarmac but later becoming a rough enclosed track. At a fork in front of a house, take the left-hand track which steadily descends and, where the track ends, keep ahead through a gate.

Continue in the same direction across a field, heading down to climb a stile in

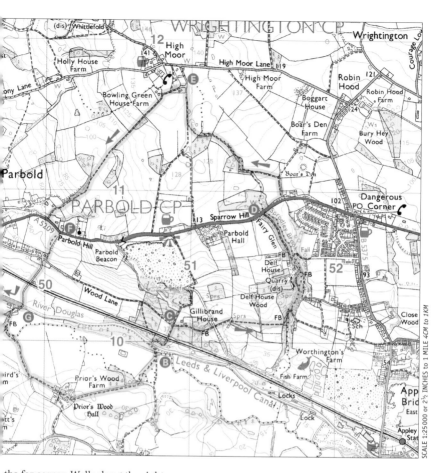

the far corner. Walk along the right edge of the next field, climb another stile and keep ahead through trees to the main road again. Turn left and, at a public footpath sign, turn right **F** over a stile and walk along the right edge of a field, descending quite steeply to a stile. After climbing it, turn right along a tarmac track but, almost immediately, turn left onto a track which heads down to a railway line. Cross the railway line very carefully, keep ahead to a canal bridge **G**, cross that and turn left down to the towpath.

Turn sharp left to pass under the bridge and follow the towpath of the Leeds and Liverpool Canal back to Parbold. At bridge 37 – just in front of an 18th-century windmill – head up to the road and turn right over the bridge to return to the start. ●

Fairy Glen

Gorple Road and Towneley Park

Start	Hurstwood
Distance	6 miles (9.7km)
Approximate time	3 hours
Parking	Hurstwood
Refreshments	Pubs at Worsthorne, pubs at Mereclough, café in Towneley Park
Ordnance Survey maps	Landranger 103 (Blackburn & Burnley), Outdoor Leisure 21 (South Pennines)

It is difficult to believe that this splendid and almost completely rural walk is on the edge of Burnley and – at one point – no more than 1 mile (1.6km) from the town centre. The route starts among the moors to the east of Burnley, uses a short stretch of an old trans-Pennine pack-horse trail, goes through the attractive villages of Hurstwood and Worsthorne and then descends into Towneley Park. From there it continues through the park and passes through two more villages before returning to the start. There is plenty of scenic variety and historic interest, but no difficult or strenuous sections and a minimum of suburban road walking.

From the car park walk back along the track, crossing the River Brun, into Hurstwood, a picturesque hamlet of old stone cottages. The most prominent building is the late 16th-century Hurstwood Hall. Almost opposite is Spenser's Cottage, of similar age and reputedly the home for a while of the Elizabethan poet, Edmund Spenser, author of *The Faerie Queene* and a contemporary of Shakespeare.

Immediately turn right to pass in front of cottages, climb a stile, keep ahead along a walled grassy track and continue along a path which heads uphill above the river to a kissing gate on the edge of woodland. Go through, walk along an enclosed path by the left

edge of the trees, ascending a flight of steps, climb a stile and the path turns first left and then right to another stile. Climb it, turn left Ⓐ onto a path across rough grassy moorland, climbing three stiles, and after the third one, bear slightly left and climb another stile in the left field corner onto a broad walled track Ⓑ.

This is Gorple Road, an old pack-horse trail across the Pennines, and you turn left along it into the village of Worsthorne. At a T-junction turn left through the village, passing the Victorian church, and just after the post office, turn right along Hall Street Ⓒ. Where the road ends, keep ahead

along a track, climb a waymarked stile, walk along the left edge of a field and bear left to continue gently downhill across the field, making for another waymarked stile to the right of a bungalow. Climb it, walk along a tarmac path, which bends right to emerge onto the end of a road, and follow the road to a T-junction.

Turn right along Lindsay Park to another T-junction, and turn left heading down to cross a bridge over the River Brun. At a public footpath sign to Brunshaw Road, turn left Ⓓ to pass

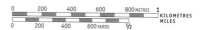

beside a barrier. Walk along a path enclosed by garden fences to a road, cross over and continue along an enclosed path to a stile. Climb it, head uphill, climb a stile at the top and keep ahead to climb another one. Continue along the enclosed path to a road, turn left, then right into Springwood Road **E** and take the second turning on the left (still Springwood Road).

The road bends right and now becomes Deer Park Road, an attractive, tree-lined drive which descends through a golf course, passes Deer Pond Local Nature Reserve and continues through Towneley Park and over the River Calder to Towneley Hall **F**. This impressive late medieval house, reconstructed in the early 19th century, was the home of the Towneley family from the 13th century until 1902. It now belongs to Burnley Council and is a museum and art gallery.

From the hall, retrace your steps along the drive to a crossroads and turn right along another drive, passing beside a car park. After crossing a bridge over a burn, keep ahead along a track across a playing field to a kissing gate. Go through, continue first along the track and later along a path through trees and go through a kissing gate onto a road in the village of Cliviger. Keep ahead and, immediately after crossing Cliviger Mill Bridge over the Calder, turn left through a gate **G**.

Walk along a track and, at a fork in front of an old farmhouse, take the left-hand track. Go through a gate and bear left to climb a stile. Turn right along a path which passes to the left of farm buildings, bear slightly right and follow a narrow grassy path gently uphill across a large field to a stile. Climb it, bear left across a field, continue along its left edge and go through a gate in the corner. Walk along the left field edge, climb a ladder stile, keep ahead and go through a gate in the field corner. Continue along the right edge of the next field, climb a stile, bear slightly left across a field, skirting a fence corner, and go through a gate onto a road **H**.

Turn right if you want to visit the pubs in Mereclough; otherwise turn left and, at a public footpath sign, turn right through a squeezer stile. Walk across a field, climb a stone stile and turn right along a walled track. Just after passing a farm – and by the entrance to Rock Water Bird Centre – turn left **J** along a path which descends and continues through trees to cross a footbridge. Head uphill into Hurstwood opposite Spenser's Cottage, turn right and right again over the bridge to return to the car park. ●

Near Towneley Park

Jumbles Country Park to Hall i'th Wood

Start	Jumbles Country Park Information Centre
Distance	6½ miles (10.5km)
Approximate time	3½ hours
Parking	Jumbles Country Park, Waterfold car park
Refreshments	Kiosk at Jumbles Country Park Information Centre, tearoom at Turton Tower, pub and teashop at Last Drop Village, pub at Eagley
Ordnance Survey maps	Landranger 109 (Manchester, Bolton & Warrington), Explorer 287 (West Pennine Moors)

There is much scenic variety and considerable historic interest on this walk. After an opening stroll beside the attractive Jumbles Reservoir, the route heads across to Turton Tower and on across fields to Last Drop Village. It then continues through the wooded valley of Eagley Brook to Hall i'th Wood, closely associated with the Industrial Revolution and the Lancashire cotton industry. More field paths bring you to Bromley Cross and from there a walk across meadows and through woodland leads back to the start.

Jumbles Country Park is based around Jumbles Reservoir, built in 1971 and one of a number constructed in the Bradshaw valley to the north of Bolton.

🖌 Begin by heading alongside the reservoir on the left and turn left to cross a footbridge near its northern end Ⓐ. At a fork, take the right hand path, signposted to Turton Tower, and climb steps to enter woodland. Climb a stile on the far side of the trees, keep ahead over a brow and climb another stile onto a road.

Turn left and, after 200 yds (183m), turn right along a tree-lined track Ⓑ which passes to the left of Turton Tower. This was originally a peel tower, built in the 15th century as a defence against Scottish incursions, but

enlarged and modernised in the Tudor and Stuart periods and again in the Victorian era. Much of the panelling was brought here from nearby demolished houses and there is a fine collection of paintings and furniture.

Cross a castellated railway bridge - built to harmonise with the tower - keep ahead along a tree-lined path to a T-junction and turn left over a stile Ⓒ. Walk along the left edge of a field, alongside a wire fence, and go through a kissing gate in the field corner. Continue across Turton golf course, following a line of yellow-topped marker posts through a group of young trees and over a brow, to reach a track at a bend. Keep ahead, down into a dip and up again, go through a gate into

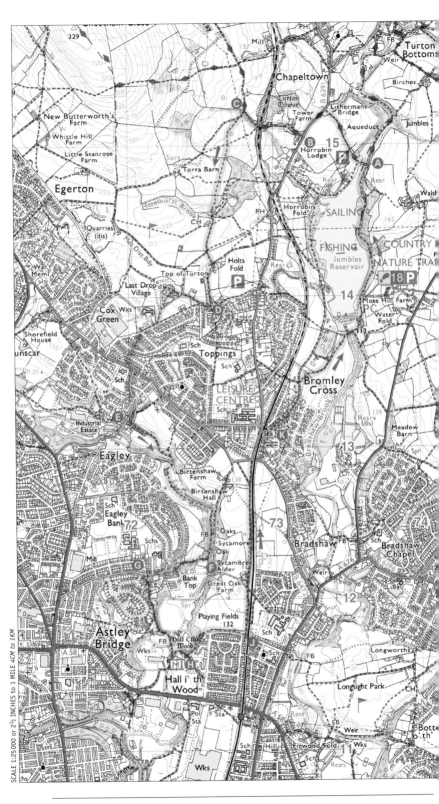

the golf club car park and continue along a tarmac track to a road  **D**.

Turn right and, at a public footpath sign, bear right along a track to Last Drop Village. This purpose-built complex is a collection of old farm buildings that were restored and converted into a traditional English village in the 1960s by a local businessman. There is a pub, hotel, teashop, galleries and shops. Keep ahead along a tarmac path through the village, turn left at a sign 'Leisure Club and Reception', pass between the hotel buildings into the car park and keep ahead along a drive down to a road.

Turton Tower

Turn right and look out for a public footpath sign in a hedge where you turn left along an enclosed tarmac path. Head downhill – crossing several suburban roads – and continue along a short stretch of road (Blair Street) to a main road.

Turn left, take the first turning on the right (Hough Lane), head downhill and, at a public footpath sign, turn left **E** along a track (Paper Mill Road), passing a row of terrace cottages. To the right, the imposing redbrick paper mill can be seen. Just beyond the end of the houses, pass beside a barrier and walk along a path which gently descends to a T-junction. Turn left by Eagley Brook, bear right to cross a footbridge over it and follow the path ahead uphill.

The next part of the walk is fairly tortuous as there are a lot of paths and path junctions – not always clear – and the route directions need to be followed carefully. Turn left off the main path onto a path that passes to the right of a small pool and continues gently uphill across the wooded hillside to emerge into a small, open grassy area. Bear left to walk beside a wire fence on the right. At a fork, take the left-hand path into the trees and look out for the next fork where you take the left-hand narrow path which heads downhill and continues along a ledge above Eagley Brook. The path gradually descends, then keeps along the top of an embankment above the brook and goes down steps to a footbridge. Do not cross it but keep ahead and pass beside a barrier onto a track **F**.

Turn right along this cobbled track, heading uphill to a road. Turn right, keep ahead at a junction into Astley Bridge and, just after passing a chapel on the left – and opposite Hill Cot Road – turn left along an enclosed track **G**.

0 200 400 600 800 METRES 1
0 200 400 600 YARDS ½
KILOMETRES
MILES

Jumbles Reservoir

The track continues through woodland high above Eagley Brook, bears left downhill and, in front of a gate, bear right to continue along an enclosed path.

Cross a footbridge over a tributary brook, keep ahead steeply uphill through trees to a T-junction and turn left along an uphill cobbled path to Hall i'th Wood. This timber-framed, late medieval manor house was altered and enlarged in the 16th and 17th centuries and restored at the end of the 19th century by Lord Leverhulme. Its main claim to fame is that it was here that Samuel Crompton developed the spinning mule in 1779, an event which helped to revolutionise the Lancashire cotton industry.

Where the path bears right by the corner of the hall, turn left **H**, pass beside a barrier and and walk along the left edge of a grassy area by houses. Pass beside another barrier and keep ahead along an enclosed path which emerges into a playing field. Turn right along the right edge of the field and follow the edge to the left **J** to reach a footbridge over the railway line.

Continue along the edge of the playing field, parallel to the railway, and in the field corner, keep ahead to pass beside a barrier onto a cobbled track. Cross it, take the path ahead and continue in a straight line along the right edge of fields – still beside the railway – eventually to emerge onto a road in Bromley Cross.

Turn right to pass under a railway bridge, take the first turning on the left (Shady Lane) and bear right to continue along Grange Road **K**. At a public footpath sign, turn right through a hedge gap and, at a fork immediately ahead, take the left-hand path to continue across a meadow and into woodland. Climb a stile at the far end of the wood, keep ahead across rough grassland and the path heads up to a T-junction.

Turn right onto a well-defined path and cross a footbridge over Bradshaw Brook. Climb steps on the other side and keep ahead, in the Jumbles Country Park direction, climbing more steps to emerge into a car park. Continue through it to return to the starting point of the walk. ●

Lytham and the Ribble Estuary

Start	Lytham, The Green
Distance	7½ miles (12.1km)
Approximate time	3½ hours
Parking	Lytham
Refreshments	Pubs and cafés at Lytham
Ordnance Survey maps	Landranger 102 (Preston & Blackpool), Explorer 286 (Blackpool & Preston)

From Lytham's spacious Green overlooking the Ribble estuary, the route heads inland, mainly along roads, lanes, tree-lined avenues and field paths, before returning to the estuary. The last 3 miles (4.8km) is by the shore above the Ribble marshes, passing through former docks and boatyards. There are wide and extensive views over the flat and fertile lands of the Fylde and across the estuary, with nearby Blackpool Tower sometimes in sight.

It was in the late 18th century that Lytham started to develop as a fashionable resort on the Fylde coast and with its old cottages, handsome Georgian houses, good selection of restaurants and coffee shops and spacious green, it still retains an air of elegance and dignity. The walk starts by the lifeboat station on Lytham Green, not far from the early 19th-century windmill, the town's best-known landmark, although no longer in use.

Head away from the shore, cross the main road, walk along Bath Street and turn left along Clifton Street into the town centre. In Clifton Square turn right along Park Street, cross a railway bridge, pass the entrance to Lytham Hall and continue along Ballam Road. At a road junction by a small triangular green, turn right **A** along a

Fylde landscape near Lytham

delightful tree-lined drive – Green Drive – which emerges onto a road **B**. Turn left and where the road bends left just after crossing a bridge, turn right **C** along the drive to Eastham Hall caravan park.

Opposite a house, a public footpath sign directs you to the right onto a tree-lined path which curves left and continues to a stile. Climb it, cross a railway track, climb the stile opposite and walk along the left edge of a field. Climb a stile, keep ahead to climb another one in the field corner and turn right onto a track which bends left and continues to a lane. Turn left and follow the lane to a T-junction in the village of Wrea Brook.

Turn left and, by the first house on the right, turn sharp right onto a path above the brook **D**. Climb a stile, bear left and head diagonally across a field. In the field corner, pass under an arch between fence posts, keep to the right of a barn and climb a ladder stile onto a lane. Turn right, follow the lane around several bends and, where it peters out above the marshes, turn right **E** onto a track to join the Lancashire Coastal Way.

After climbing a stile, the route continues along a raised embankment to a kissing gate. Go through, keep ahead and, in front of a gate, turn right down to a stile for a short detour inland. After climbing the

stile, walk along a track to the main road, turn left over a bridge and immediately turn left again **F**. Continue above a brook on the left and, after climbing a stile, you rejoin the embankment. Climb another stile, continue along the embankment, climb two more stiles in quick succession and you later follow the curve of the

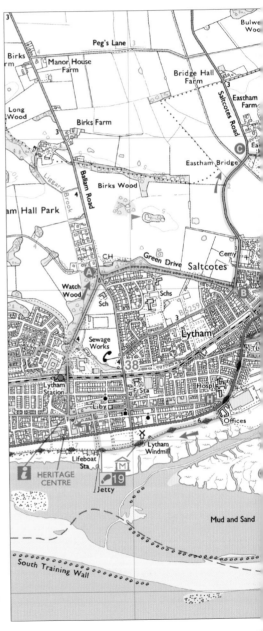

embankment to the right alongside a creek. Climb a stile and keep ahead to climb another one onto the main road again.

Turn left, at a public footpath sign turn left again 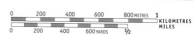 **G** onto a track and pass through a boatyard. At a waymarked post, continue along a path which turns right and keeps beside another creek.

Descend steps to the main road once more and turn left into Lytham. At the Green, turn left along the edge of it **H** and turn right to continue above the Ribble marshes, passing the windmill, to return to the start. ●

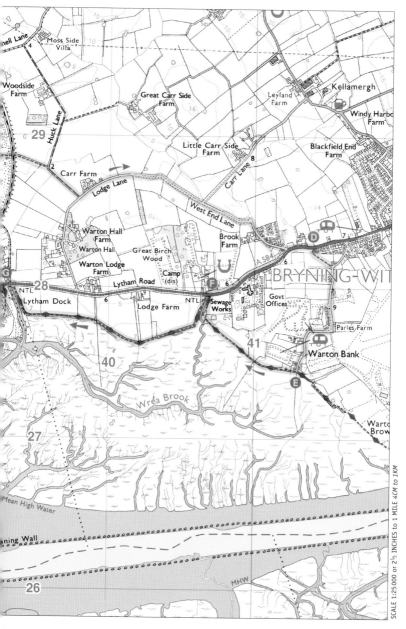

Holcombe Moor and the Peel Tower

Start	Ramsbottom, Market Place
Distance	6½ miles (10.5km)
Approximate time	3½ hours
Parking	Ramsbottom
Refreshments	Pubs and cafés at Ramsbottom, pub at Holcombe
Ordnance Survey maps	Landranger 109 (Manchester, Bolton & Warrington), Explorer 287 (West Pennine Moors)

A pleasant opening stretch by the River Irwell is followed by a steady climb through the wooded Buckden Clough onto Holcombe Moor. The route continues across the open and breezy expanses of the moor to the well-known landmark of the Peel Tower before descending to Holcombe and on down to Ramsbottom. There is some rough moorland walking and expect muddy conditions in places but the route is fairly clear and easy to follow. There are no steep gradients and the views across the moor are superb.

Note that Holcombe Moor is an Army Firing Range and is closed when firing is in progress. This is indicated by the flying of red flags. Information can be obtained by phoning 01204 882991

Originally a small market town on the River Irwell, Ramsbottom developed into a textile town during the Industrial Revolution. It is now becoming a tourist centre and has a station on the East Lancashire Railway, a preserved steam railway that runs through the Irwell valley between the towns of Bury and Rawtenstall.

Begin by walking down Bridge Street, keep ahead over a level crossing, cross the bridge over the River Irwell and take the first turning on the left (Kenyon Street) **A**. At a public footpath sign, turn right onto a tarmac path between a factory fence on the left and a wooded slope on the right, go through a kissing gate, turn left and then bear right across a meadow to the riverbank. Keep beside it, climb a stile, cross a footbridge over a stream, go through a kissing gate and continue along the right edge of a meadow. Go through a double gate, bear left down a track to a kissing gate, go through that and continue along the track, rejoining the Irwell, to a bridge.

Turn left over it, turn right **B**, at a public footpath sign, and walk along the other bank of the river, passing in front of houses and between gardens and allotments. At the next public footpath sign, turn left away from the river, pass in front of a row of cottages, go under a railway bridge and head up to a road. Turn right, passing between a former mill complex, and the road later becomes a wooded track which you follow to the left, passing to the right of cottages. Head gently uphill along an enclosed track which keeps by the right edge of a narrow, wooded ravine and climb a stile to enter the National Trust's Stubbins Estate. Continue gently uphill, cross the brook, climb above the left side of it and, at a fork about 50 yds (46m) before reaching a stile, take the right-hand lower path which leads down to a footbridge. Turn right over it, head up steps – bearing slightly right away from the brook – and continue beside an embankment on the right to a stile.

Climb it to emerge onto the open moorland, keep ahead, turn right over a stile and turn left onto a track. At a

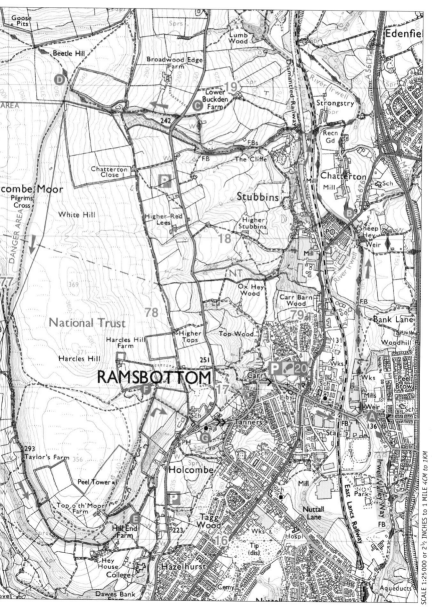

Holcombe Moor

T-junction, turn left, follow a track up to a road, **C** go through the gate opposite and continue steadily uphill, skirting the right edge of woodland. Climb a ladder stile, keep ahead as far as the corner of the wall on the left, bear left **D** and head up to an Army Firing Range warning notice. *Do not proceed if red flags are flying.*

Bear left again and continue along a fairly clear – though likely to be muddy – track across Holcombe Moor. The track follows a line of red and white posts and warning signs and passes the Pilgrims' Cross, on the site of a much older cross which marked a resting place for pilgrims on their way to Whalley Abbey. The track eventually descends by Holcombe Head and continues, beside a broken down wall on the right, to a stile. Climb it – and another – and the track curves left around the southern end of the moor to a gate. Go through, walk along an enclosed track, pass one farm and, just before reaching a second one – where there are stiles on both sides of the track – climb the stile on the left **E**. Head

steeply uphill, by a fence on the right and climb a stile onto a track. Turn left, still heading uphill, follow the track around a right bend and keep ahead to the Peel Tower. This was erected in 1852 to commemorate Sir Robert Peel's Repeal of the Corn Laws which reduced the price of food for the local workers. Peel came from this area.

Continue ahead along a track, go through a kissing gate and look out for a ladder stile in the wall on the right **F**. Climb it and head downhill along the right edge of a field. Climb a stone stile, continue downhill and, in the field corner, climb another stone stile onto a track. Turn left and, almost immediately, turn right down an enclosed walled path to a road. The pub at Holcombe is about 200 yds (183m) to the right.

Cross over and continue down a cobbled path to emerge onto a lower lane opposite Holcombe's Victorian church **G**. Turn left downhill, bear left at a T-junction, follow the lane around a right bend and continue down into Ramsbottom town centre.

Crawshawbooth and Lumb

Crawshawbooth and Lumb

Start	Crawshawbooth
Distance	7 miles (11.3km)
Approximate time	3½ hours
Parking	Roadside parking at Crawshawbooth
Refreshments	Pubs and cafés at Crawshawbooth, pub at Lumb
Ordnance Survey maps	Landranger 103 (Blackburn & Burnley) & Outdoor Leisure 21 (South Pennines)

Almost the whole of this invigorating walk is over the open, grassy moorlands of the Forest of Rossendale to the north of the Irwell valley. The views are extensive and, just after the start, the route passes an 18th-century Baptist chapel. There are no steep gradients but there is some rough moorland walking, parts of which are likely to be muddy. Do not attempt this walk in bad weather, especially misty conditions, unless you are able to navigate by using a compass.

The walk starts in the centre of Crawshawbooth by the large and imposing Victorian church. Walk northwards along the main road (A682), turn right into Goodshaw Lane **A** and follow the lane uphill for just over ½ mile (800m) to Goodshaw chapel.

This Baptist chapel, built in 1760, is a rare example of an early Nonconformist place of worship which has survived virtually unaltered.

Continue along the lane and, just before it bends right, turn right **B** and climb a stile to join the Rossendale Way.

Rossendale moorland

Follow a path gently uphill over the grassy moorland, keeping by a fence on the right, and turn right to climb a stile. Keep ahead uphill, climb another stile and continue beside a wall on the right – Clowbridge Reservoir is seen below on the left – to a gate at a six-way junction of paths. Go through and bear slightly right along a path which continues over the bleak and open moorland. On reaching a wall, turn first left and then immediately right to go through a gap in it and keep by a wall on the right, going through gaps in several broken-down walls.

At a crossroads of paths and tracks, turn right over a stile **C**. Just to the left is a stone cross, erected in 1902. Walk along a path by a wall on the left and, after crossing a stony track, the path heads gently downhill to a stile. Climb it, keep ahead along a track, go through a gate, cross a track and continue to a T-junction to the left of a farm. Go through the gate in front, continue gently downhill and go through another

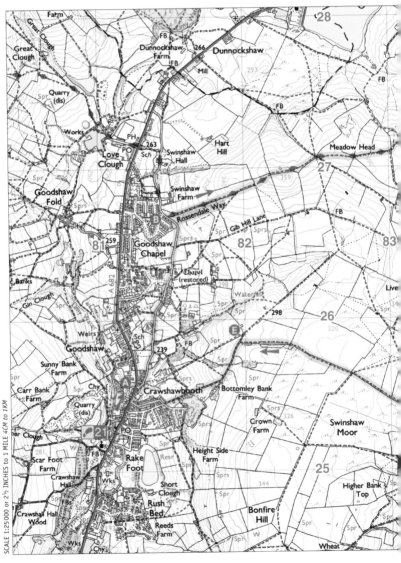

gate. Keep ahead along the right edge of a field, above a stream on the right, and the path curves right to cross the stream.

Immediately, go through a gate, continue gently uphill, go through another gate and keep ahead to a T-junction where you turn left over a stile. Bear right through a gate, walk along a path by a wall on the left and,

after going through the next gate, the path becomes enclosed. Go through a gate, follow the path around a left bend – it now becomes a track – and head downhill, going through another gate. Keep ahead to emerge onto the end of a road and continue along it into Lumb. At a T-junction, turn right and, after a right curve, bear right **D** onto an ascending tarmac track beside a high churchyard wall on the right.

Pass to the left of the cruciform, 19th-century church, built in a neo-Norman style instead of the usual neo-Gothic style. It is now derelict. At a fork, take the right-hand track which winds uphill towards a farm and turn right in front of the gates still on a tarmac track. The track curves left to a stile. Climb it, at a footpath post turn right downhill alongside a wire fence and, after climbing another stile, head quite steeply up an embankment to go through a gate at the corner of farm buildings. Keep ahead along the right edge of a field and, at a wall gap, turn left to continue along the right field edge, by a broken-down wall on the right.

Go through a gap and head in a straight line across Swinshaw Moor, keeping by either a wall or fence on the left. After climbing a stile, the route continues by a wall on the right. Climb a stile and, where the wall shortly peters out, keep ahead to climb another stile. Continue by a fence on the right, heading gently downhill, and go through a kissing gate on to a track **E**. Turn left downhill along this enclosed track and, at a three-way fork, take the right-hand track which continues down into Crawshawbooth.

At a public footpath sign at the beginning of the houses, turn right along a road which bends left and continues steeply down to the main road. Turn left to return to the start. ●

Scorton, Grize Dale and Nicky Nook

Start	Scorton Picnic Site, about 1½ miles (2.4km) north of Scorton village
Distance	6½ miles (10.5km)
Approximate time	3½ hours
Parking	Scorton Picnic Site
Refreshments	Cafés at Scorton
Ordnance Survey maps	Landranger 102 (Preston & Blackpool), Outdoor Leisure 41 (Forest of Bowland & Ribblesdale)

This walk on the western edge of the Forest of Bowland provides you with magnificent views for relatively little effort. An opening stroll across fields brings you into the pleasant village of Scorton. From there the route continues up to Grize Dale for a walk through the beautiful, well-wooded valley to Grizedale Reservoir. A fairly steep but short ascent then leads to the summit of Nicky Nook. Although only 705 ft (215m) high, the views from here are superb and extensive. After the descent, tracks and field paths lead back to the start. Parts of the walk may well be muddy, especially on the latter stages.

Turn right out of the car park along the lane and, at a public footpath sign to Park Lane, turn left over a stile and walk along a tree-lined track. The River Wyre is beyond the embankment on the right. Look out for where a public footpath sign directs you to turn left over a stile, keep ahead to climb another one and continue along a narrow fence-lined path, parallel to the M6 over to the left.

Climb a stile, walk along the right edge of a field, by a brook on the right, climb another stile and keep ahead across a field corner, rejoining the field edge and continuing by it to a stile. Climb it, keep ahead to a footbridge, turn left over it and turn right along the right edge of a field. To the right is a fine view of Scorton Lake. At a public footpath sign, turn right over a stile, recross the brook and turn left along a narrow enclosed path. The path bends left to cross the brook once more and continues through trees to emerge onto a road **A**.

Turn right into Scorton, continue through the village and, soon after passing the church on the left, turn left along Tithe Barn Lane **B**. After passing under the motorway, the lane heads uphill, bending first right and then left. Ignore a Wyre Way sign on the right but, at the next public footpath sign, where the lane curves left, bear right along a tarmac drive. Climb a stone stile to the left of a cattle grid, climb two more in quick succession and head

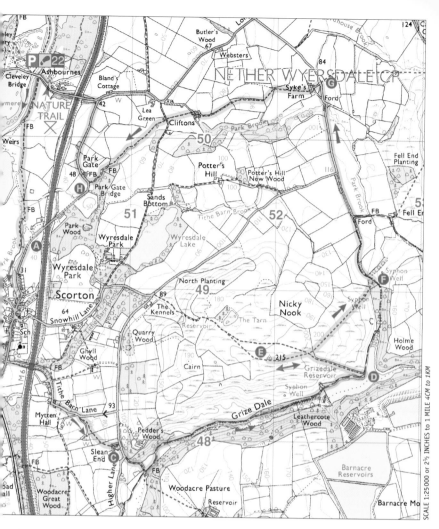

SCALE 1:25000 or 2½ INCHES to 1 MILE 4CM to 1KM

| 0 | 200 | 400 | 600 | 800 METRES | 1 |
| 0 | 200 | 400 | 600 YARDS | ½ | KILOMETRES MILES |

uphill across a field, making for a stile in the corner of a wire fence. After climbing it, keep in the same direction across the next field towards a barn but, before reaching the field edge, turn left and continue up to climb a stile onto a lane.

Turn right downhill along this narrow lane and, where it bends right, keep ahead through a kissing gate C. There is an information board here about Grize Dale as well as a public footpath sign to Grizedale Valley. The path heads downhill by woodland on the left and then bears right across a field to a stile. Climb it and turn left to continue along an attractive, tree-lined

track through Grize Dale, keeping by the brook on the right. Nicky Nook can be seen to the left. The track later narrows to a path and climbs steadily between trees and gorse bushes above the brook to a kissing gate.

Go through and keep along the left side of Grizedale Reservoir, constructed in 1866 to provide water for the Fylde. Just after a slight left bend, turn left over a stone stile D, at a public footpath sign 'Nicky Nook for Scorton', head steeply uphill between bracken – there are steps in places – and continue along the broad ridge to the triangulation pillar on the summit **E**. From here the magnificent views include the Fylde, Morecambe Bay, Heysham power station, the outline of the Lakeland fells, the Bowland fells and the West Pennine moors.

Retrace your steps and, at a fork, instead of taking the right-hand path that you came up, take the left-hand path to a ladder stile. Climb it, keep ahead, passing a stone pillar, and descend to a footpath post. Continue past it across a boggy area and then follow a track down to climb a stile and reach a T-junction. Turn left **F** along a track and, after going through a kissing gate, continue along a lane. About 200 yds (183m) after crossing a footbridge beside a ford, turn left **G**, at a public footpath sign, along a farm track. Follow the yellow waymarks through the farm buildings to a gate. Go through, walk across a field, later keeping by a wire fence on the right, and climb a stile in the corner.

Bear slightly left and head gently uphill across the next field over a slight brow to a stile. Climb it, keep along the right edge of a field to a farm, again follow the waymarks through the farm buildings and, almost immediately after turning right onto a tarmac drive, turn left over a stile. Walk across a field, climb a stile on the far side, turn right along a tarmac track and, after a few yards, turn left over a stile. Bear slightly left across a field, making for a stile on the far side. After climbing it, continue in the same direction across the next field and climb a stile in a wire fence.

Keep ahead to climb another stile, walk along the left edge of a field, by a brook on the left, and turn left to cross a footbridge over the brook. Continue between the brook on the right and woodland on the left, recross the brook to reach a stile, climb it and turn right **H** along a road, parallel to the M6. Turn left into Cleveley Bank Lane and cross the motorway to return to the starting point of the walk. ●

View over the Fylde near Scorton

Douglas Valley and Ashurst's Beacon

Start	Beacon Country Park Visitor Centre
Distance	8 miles (12.9km)
Approximate time	4 hours
Parking	Beacon Country Park
Refreshments	Pub and café at Visitor Centre, pub at Roby Mill, pub at Bank Top, pubs at Gathurst, pubs at Appley Bridge, pub just below Ashurst's Beacon
Ordnance Survey maps	Landranger 108 (Liverpool, Southport & Wigan), Explorer 285 (Southport & Chorley)

Beacon Country Park and the nearby Ashurst's Beacon occupy a broad ridge, one of the westerly outliers of the Pennines, that lies between Skelmersdale and Wigan. It commands extensive views over the Douglas valley to Pendle Hill and the West Pennine moors, and across the flat lands of West Lancashire to Southport and the coast. The route descends into the Douglas valley and continues through it along the towpath of the Leeds and Liverpool Canal to Appley Bridge. From there a lengthy but relatively easy and gradual ascent leads up to Ashurst's Beacon and back to the start.

Facing the Visitor Centre, turn left and take the path which leads off from the far end of the car park. After bearing left and going up steps, turn right to a T-junction, turn left up to a stile and climb it onto a road **A**. Cross over and take the path opposite which turns sharp left around the edge of a garden. It continues gently downhill, first along the left edge of a field, then through a narrow belt of trees, along the left edge of another field and finally along the edge of a golf course.

Where you see a stile and lane over to the left, bear right across the corner of the golf course and, at the edge of trees, turn right to pick up a definite path and walk along the left edge of a field.

Continue across another part of the golf course and then keep ahead along the right edge of a field. In the field corner, follow an enclosed path first to the left and then to the right to reach a road at Roby Mill. Turn right, turn left by the Fox Inn along School Lane and, at the end of a row of bungalows, turn left and descend to cross a brook.

Continue uphill to reach a road just to the right of the Star Inn, turn right **B** and the road becomes a rough track. In front of the gates to Ayrefield House, bear right alongside the house, turn right to go through a gate and continue along a broad path which turns left and heads downhill, later keeping by the right edge of a line of trees, to a stile.

After climbing it, continue beside a wire fence down to the River Douglas and turn right through woodland bordering it. Turn left to cross a footbridge over a brook and walk along a wide path which rejoins the river and passes under the M6 viaduct to reach a road at Gathurst.

Turn left, passing under a railway bridge and over the river, and at the canal bridge, turn left down steps onto the towpath **C**. You now keep beside the Leeds and Liverpool Canal as far as Appley Bridge, a distance of nearly 2 miles (3.2km). In front of the bridge, bear left through a parking area to a road, turn left to recross the river and immediately turn right onto an enclosed path alongside it **D**.

The path later leaves the river and bears left across the field to cross a stream. Turn left and follow the right bank of the stream, passing to the right of a farm, up to a lane **E**. Turn left and

Ashurst's Beacon

take the first track on the right which winds up to another lane. Turn right, continue uphill along this narrow lane, ignore the first public footpath sign but turn right up steps at the second one **F**. Keep along the right edge of a field, turn left in the field corner and continue as far as a footbridge below on the right.

Cross it, turn left to climb a stile and turn left again along the left edge of a field. Turn left over another stile, continue through trees and, when you see Ashurst's Beacon over to the right, make your way across to it. This is an old signal tower and the views from here – over the Douglas valley to Pendle Hill and the West Pennine moors – are spectacular. At the beacon, turn left, head down to rejoin the previous path and continue through trees and over a stile onto a road.

Turn left and just after passing in front of the Ashurst's Beacon Inn, turn right **G** onto a path through woodland. Follow this well-waymarked path through trees and across a golf course to return to the Visitor Centre. ●

Hodder and Dunsop Valleys

Start	Dunsop Bridge
Distance	7½ miles (12.1km)
Approximate time	4 hours
Parking	Dunsop Bridge
Refreshments	None
Ordnance Survey maps	Landranger 103 (Blackburn & Burnley), Outdoor Leisure 41 (Forest of Bowland & Ribblesdale)

The walk is in the heart of the majestic and lonely terrain of the Forest of Bowland and there are magnificent views, both over the Hodder and Dunsop valleys and of the dramatic outlines of the Bowland fells. Easy and relaxing riverside walking comes at the start and finish but, in between, the route goes across some rough moorland and there are several moderate climbs. Although the paths and tracks are reasonably well-defined in most places, there is one short stretch across open, pathless moorland and it is advisable not to attempt this walk in bad weather – particularly in misty conditions – unless experienced in such conditions and able to navigate by using a compass.

The small village of Dunsop Bridge lies at the gateway to the Trough of Bowland, the traditional route across the fells between Clitheroe and Lancaster. It has acquired a new fame as the nearest settlement to the exact geographical centre of Great Britain and

Bowland fells near Dunsop Bridge

a telephone box on the green commemorates this.

🖊 Turn left out of the car park and where the road bends left, bear right through gates and walk along the tree-lined drive of Thorneyholme Hall. Cross a bridge over the River Hodder Ⓐ – near its confluence with the Dunsop – immediately turn right through a gate and walk along a riverside path. The path joins a track but where the track bears left after going through a gate, keep beside the Hodder, climbing several stiles, until the river bends right. Continue ahead over a stile, walk across a field, climb another stile and head over a slight rise to Burholme Farm. After joining a track, go through a gate into the farmyard, cross a foot-bridge over a beck and follow the track to the right, passing in front of the farm-

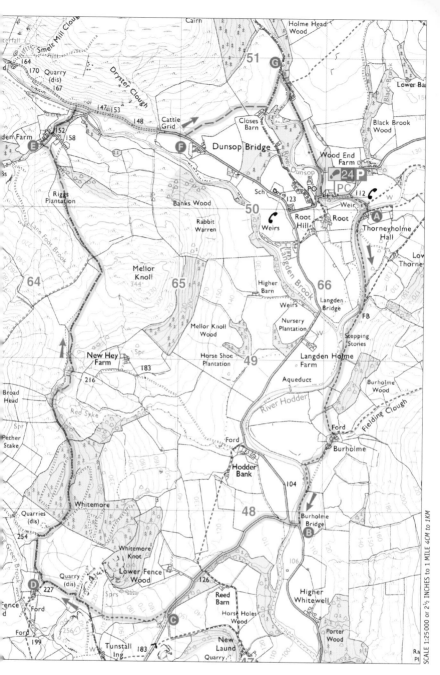

house. Go through another gate and follow the track to Burholme Bridge **B**. Turn right over the bridge – to the left the church and inn at Whitewell can be seen – and keep ahead along the lane signposted to Chipping. The lane winds steadily uphill and, just before reaching the end of a belt of woodland on the left, bear right **C** along a track, at a public footpath sign, to a gate. Go through, continue uphill along a grassy track and go through another gate to shortly join a tarmac track.

Hodder valley near Dunsop Bridge

Follow it to where it swings left towards a farm and here turn right **D** onto another tarmac track which curves right beside a fence on the left and heads up towards conifers. Where the track bends left, turn right – at a blue-waymarked post – onto a grassy track which bears left and continues up to a gate at the corner of the conifer plantation. Go through, continue through the plantation, go through another gate at the far end and head downhill along an enclosed path. The path continues through trees – some white-waymarked posts show the way – and over to the right there are stunning views over the Hodder valley and the encircling fells. Head up up to a stile, climb it, keep by a wall on the right and turn right over a ladder stile in that wall.

Bear right and head across rough, open moorland, making for the left shoulder of a hill – Mellor Knoll – where you bear left along a track to another ladder stile. Climb it, head downhill and where the track peters out, bear right away from the wall and continue downhill across grass, making for the left edge of trees. In front is a superb view looking towards the Trough of Bowland. Climb a ladder stile and turn right to continue downhill beside a wall, bearing left away from it to climb another ladder stile in front of a farmhouse **E**. Turn right along a track, crossing Hareden Brook twice and Langden Brook, to emerge onto the Trough of Bowland road and then turn right.

Shortly after a cattle grid, turn left **F** through a gate, at a public bridleway sign, and head up over a slight rise. Walk towards the farm buildings ahead, go through a gate, keep ahead over a stile and continue across rough grass to a tarmac track. Turn left, turn right to cross a footbridge over the River Dunsop **G** and turn right again onto a riverside path.

After climbing a stile, bear right to pass in front of a row of cottages and continue along a tarmac track. Go through a gate, follow the track to the road in Dunsop Bridge and turn left to the start.

Ribchester, Stonyhurst and the River Ribble

Start	Ribchester
Distance	9½ miles (15.3km) Shorter version 8 miles (12.9km)
Approximate time	5 hours (4 hours for shorter walk)
Parking	Ribchester
Refreshments	Pubs at Ribchester, pubs at Hurst Green
Ordnance Survey maps	Landranger 103 (Blackburn & Burnley), Explorer 287 (West Pennine Moors)

There is considerable historic interest and plenty of variety on this energetic walk amidst some of the finest scenery in the Ribble valley. Historic features include the Roman remains at Ribchester, almshouses and medieval chapel at Stydd and the great Elizabethan house at Stonyhurst. The route also takes in superb woodland, streams, magnificent views of Pendle Hill and an attractive riverside stretch. Route finding is fairly complex, especially between points C and D where the directions need to be heeded carefully. Be prepared for muddy conditions in places after wet weather. The shorter version omits the loop around Stonyhurst.

Ribchester occupies the site of a Roman fort built in the 1st century AD. Part of the fort lies beneath the medieval church and some of it is under the river as the Ribble has changed course since Roman times. The only visible remains are those of the granary but there is a museum which displays excavated finds.

Turn right out of the car park through the village to the Ribble and turn left along a riverside path, signposted to the Roman Bath House. Immediately, there is a superb view of a great bend in the river backed by Pendle Hill. The path bends left away from the river beside a brook, passing the scanty remains of the bath house, which lay just outside the Roman fort. At a Ribble Way post, turn right and walk along a path which curves left across a field to a road. Turn right, at a T-junction turn right in front of the Ribchester Arms and take the first turning on the left (Stydd Lane) Ⓐ. After passing the dignified 18th-century almshouses at Stydd, the way continues along a rough track to Stydd Chapel. This isolated church was part of a small monastery belonging to the Knights Hospitallers which was dissolved around 1338.

Keep ahead to a farm, walk through the farmyard, go through a gate and continue along a track to a stile. Just after climbing it, bear right across a field towards a hedge corner and continue past it to a stile just to the left of the field corner. Climb it and walk along the right edge of a field, later bearing left and heading across to a stile which admits you to Duddel Wood. Continue gently downhill through the wood to cross a footbridge over Duddel Brook and turn left to walk along its right bank.

At a waymarked post, turn sharp right **B** and head uphill to a stile. Climb it, walk along the left edge of a

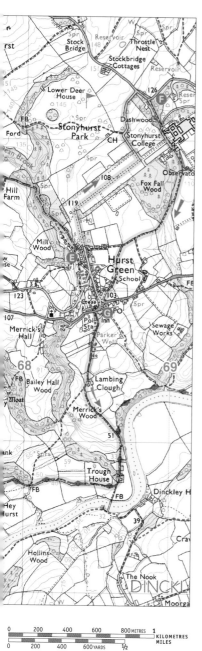

Go through a gate to the right of a house and bear left along the left edge of two fields, going over a slight brow in the second field and descending to a footbridge. Cross it, head uphill across the next field, keeping to the right of farm buildings, and climb a stile to the right of a gate. Continue across the next field, skirting the left edge of woodland and keeping parallel to the right edge, and climb a stile onto a track. Climb the stile opposite, keep ahead across two fields towards a farm, climbing another stile, and go through a gate onto a track in the corner of the second field.

Turn left through the farmyard, follow the track around a right bend, climb a stile just to the left of the track and walk across a field to a stile between two trees. Climb it and head gently uphill across the next field to a gate. Go through, keep ahead by a low embankment on the left (an old field boundary) and continue across the field to a stile. After climbing it, bear slightly left across the next field, go through a gate in front of a camping barn and go through another gate to the left of the barn onto a track ⒟.

Turn right and, at a fork, take the left hand track. The track becomes an enclosed path which descends through woodland to cross a footbridge over Dean Brook. Turn right to follow the brook through a lovely wooded gorge, later climbing above it to join a track. Walk along it to emerge onto a road on the edge of Hurst Green ⒠.

If omitting the loop around Stonyhurst, turn right and rejoin the full walk at point ⒢.

For the full walk, turn left to enter the grounds of Stonyhurst and the road bends right towards the facade of the college. Turn left in front of the college gates and follow the road around several bends to a T-junction. Turn right and, where the road bends left,

field, go through a gate, keep along the left edge of the next field and turn left through a gate onto a track in front of Dutton Hall. Turn right to a lane, turn left uphill to a T-junction, turn left and, at a public footpath sign, turn right along an enclosed track ⒞.

turn right 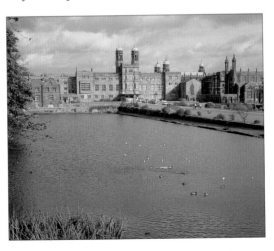, at a public footpath sign, through a gap onto a tarmac drive which passes in front of the college buildings. The Elizabethan mansion at Stonyhurst, begun in 1592, was built for the Catholic Shireburn family. It later passed to the Welds who neglected it in favour of their main residence in Dorset and it became derelict. During the French Revolution it was offered as a refuge to fleeing Jesuits who restored and extended the house, built the chapel and established it as a college.

Where this drive bends left, turn right through a gate and walk along the left edge of a field, later bearing right across the narrow field to continue by its right edge to a kissing gate. Go through, keep along the right edge of a field, go through another kissing gate and, about halfway along the edge of the next field, turn left and head across it, later by a hedge on the left. On the far side turn left through a gap, turn right alongside a wall on the right, climb a stile and keep ahead, first along a track and then a road into Hurst Green, here rejoining the short walk.

Cross over to the Shireburn Arms, turn right and at a public bridleway sign, turn left down an enclosed track beside the hotel. The track winds downhill to the Ribble and, after passing between farm buildings, it bears right to a gate. The rest of the route is on the well-waymarked Ribble Way. Go through the gate and continue across a field, keeping to the right of a gate and then along the left field edge to a stile. After climbing it, keep along the left edge of the next two fields, descending to cross a footbridge over a brook. Continue along the right edge of the next field, curving left and then heading up to go through a gate onto a track.

Turn right, almost immediately turn left through another gate, bear left and head downhill across a field to a stile. Climb it, continue downhill in the same direction to a Ribble Way post and on past it to climb another stile at the next post. Head uphill over a brow, passing a solitary tree, and continue past it, heading steeply downhill towards the river and looking out for a stile and Ribble Way sign. Turn right over the stile and walk through woodland beside the Ribble, following the river around a left bend. After crossing a footbridge over a brook, climb a ladder stile, keep ahead uphill towards trees and continue between the river and the edge of the wood-land as far as a ladder stile.

Here a Ribble Way sign directs you to turn right over it and walk along a path towards a farm. Turn left along a tarmac track, emerging onto a road by Ribchester Bridge and keep ahead. On reaching the Ribchester Arms you rejoin the outward route and retrace your steps to the start.

Stonyhurst College

Parlick and Fair Snape Fell

Start	Fell Foot, 1½ miles (2.4km) to the north west of Chipping
Distance	5½ miles (8.9km)
Approximate time	3½ hours
Parking	A few parking spaces at corner of lane just to the south of Fell Foot
Refreshments	None
Ordnance Survey maps	Landranger 102 (Preston & Blackpool), Outdoor Leisure 41 (Forest of Bowland & Ribblesdale)

There is a tremendous feeling of isolation and remoteness on this walk amidst the superlative scenery of the Forest of Bowland. An immediate short but steep climb up Parlick is followed by an easier and more gentle ascent to the 1673-ft (510m) summit of Fair Snape Fell. Both summits are magnificent all-round viewpoints. The descent is relatively easy and straightforward. Surprisingly, perhaps, some of the most difficult terrain comes on the last part of the route – between Higher Fair Snape Farm and the start – where the paths are unclear and there is rough grassland, becks to ford and some muddy stretches. It is best to choose a fine and clear day to enjoy fully the superb views throughout; the walk is not advisable in bad weather and misty conditions unless you are experienced and able to navigate by using a compass.

Begin by walking up the lane towards Fell Foot and Parlick, signposted as a No Through Road, and where the lane ends, go through a gate and climb steeply along a paved path to a fork. Take the right hand path and follow this well-worn and rocky path steeply uphill for almost ½ mile (800m) to the cairn on the summit of Parlick, 1417 ft (432m) high and a superb viewpoint **A**.

At the summit, climb a ladder stile – here entering the Fair Snape Access Area – turn right and walk beside a fence on the right. Fair Snape Fell is ahead. After heading down to an information board in a dip, keep ahead – now by a wall on the right – to a stile. Climb it and the path continues gently uphill, keeping by the wall as it curves gradually left. Later the path bears left away from the wall and heads across the open moorland to a stile.

Climb it and continue to the cairn and triangulation pillar on the summit of Fair Snape Fell **B**. At 1673 ft (510m), this is another magnificent viewpoint extending over the Bowland fells and the Fylde. Retrace your steps and, after about 200 yds (183m), look out for a grassy path on the right and turn onto it. The path curves left between shallow embankments and then twists and turns downhill across the flanks of the fell, finally bending sharply right to a ladder stile by information board 15. Turn left over the stile and turn right to continue downhill in the same direction as before to another ladder stile **C**.

Climb it and the path bends first left and then curves right to a stile. After climbing that, keep ahead to climb another one and continue downhill across a field, bending right to a stile in the field corner. Climb it, keep ahead along a track to Higher Fair Snape Farm, climb another stile and walk through the farmyard. After the next stile, the track bends left to a footpath post. Keep ahead through a gate, continue along a tarmac track and, after about 50 yds (46m), turn left through a gate **D**.

Walk along a track by the left edge of a succession of fields and over a series of stiles and look out for where you turn left over a stile in the fence on the left. Turn right to continue in the same direction along the right edge of a field,

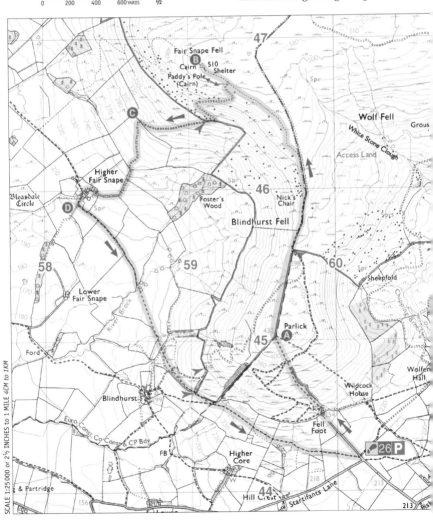

by a beck on the right, to a stile. Climb it and turn right to cross a footbridge over the infant River Brock. Turn left to a waymarked post and keep ahead across a field, veering slightly left to climb a stile in a wire fence.

Fair Snape Fell from Parlick

Continue in the same direction by the right edge of the next field, joining a track to ford a beck. Immediately, bear left off the track and head uphill across grass to a stile. Climb it, cross a track and bear right uphill along a path, initially between embankments. The path later keeps by a wire fence on the right to reach a gate by information board 13. Go through, continue across rough grass along the lower slopes of Parlick - still by a fence on the right - to the next information board and turn right over a stile.

Turn left along the left edge of a field, climb a stile, ford a beck, turn right and then bear left to head across rough pasture, keeping parallel to the base of the fell over to the left. The way now continues in more or less a straight line across four fields, climbing a succession of stiles. It is rough going and in one field there are several small becks to ford. In the final field, make for the far right hand corner and climb a stile to return to the starting point of the walk at Fell Foot. ●

Fair Snape Fell

Lune Estuary and the Lancaster Canal

Start	Lancaster, the castle. Alternatively start at Conder Green Picnic Site and follow the route directions from point(D)
Distance	11 miles (17.5km)
Approximate time	5 hours
Parking	Lancaster, or Conder Green Picnic Site
Refreshments	Pubs and cafés at Lancaster, pub at Conder Green
Ordnance Survey maps	Landrangers 97 (Kendal & Morecambe) and 102 (Preston & Blackpool), Explorer 296 (Lancaster, Morecambe & Fleetwood)

Most of the walk is beside water, either the River Lune or the Lancaster Canal. After descending from Lancaster's hilltop castle, the route keeps along the south side of the Lune estuary to Conder Green, using the track of a disused railway. A brief interlude across fields is then followed by a 4-mile (6.4-km) stretch along the towpath of the Lancaster Canal. Although a lengthy walk, the terrain is flat and the going is easy. There are superb views, initially across the estuary and Morecambe Bay to the line of the Lakeland fells, and later looking towards the Forest of Bowland. The city of Lancaster is worth exploration.

Lancaster occupies an important strategic position between the Pennines and the sea, at the lowest crossing point on the River Lune and on the main west coast route to Scotland. This is why both the Romans and Normans built fortresses here. It also affords extensive views across Morecambe Bay.

The city is dominated by the adjacent castle and priory church. The castle was founded in 1093 but little remains of the medieval structure apart from the much restored Norman keep and the gatehouse, the latter built around 1400. Over the centuries the castle has been enlarged and modernised and much of it dates from a major rebuilding in the late 18th and early 19th centuries. It is

still used as a law court and prison. The priory was founded around the same time but, in 1420, was converted into a parish church. It is a fine example of a prosperous 15th-century town church and possesses some outstanding choir stalls. During the 18th century Lancaster became an important port trading across the Atlantic with the American and West Indian colonies and there are many Georgian buildings that reflect its prosperity at the time. One of the finest of these is the Customs House passed near the start of the walk, which now houses a Maritime Museum.

Start in front of the castle gatehouse and pass to the left of it. Follow the castle walls to the right and, at a public footpath sign to St George's Quay, keep ahead along a tarmac path, passing in front of the priory. As you descend steps, there is a fine view ahead across Morecambe Bay to the Lake District. Continue downhill, descend steps, cross a tarmac track, keep ahead in front of a row of cottages and again descend steps to St George's Quay **A**.

Turn left beside the River Lune, passing former 18th-century warehouses and the elegant Customs House, and pass under Carlisle Bridge. Continue along the road for just over ¹⁄₂ mile (800m) and, where it bears left, keep ahead, at a public footpath sign to Aldcliffe Hall Lane, along a tarmac track to a stile. After climbing it, continue along a winding path beside the river, climbing another stile, and after ¹⁄₂ mile (800m) you reach a fingerpost. Turn left **B**, in the Willow Lane direction, go through a kissing gate and walk along a most attractive, tree-lined path to a crossroads **C**.

Turn right, at a public bridleway sign to Aldcliffe Hall Lane, along an enclosed track to where it ends at a Lancashire Coastal Way sign. Turn left and, at the next sign, turn right and continue along a straight, enclosed track. To the right, there are fine views across the estuary to Overton and Sunderland Point and ahead Glasson Dock can be seen. Pass under a bridge and the track eventually emerges onto the car park at the Conder Green Picnic Site **D**. Keep ahead and at a fork, take the left-hand tarmac track which curves left to a road in front of the Stork Inn.

Turn left, take the first lane on the right and, where a road comes in from the right, turn left over a stile, at a public footpath sign **E**. Walk across a field, keeping to the left of farm buildings, to a gate, go through and keep along the right edge of the next field. In the corner, turn right over a stile, turn left to cross a footbridge over a ditch and turn left along the left edge of a field.

Climb a stile in the corner and keep along the left edge of the next two fields, climbing another stile and making for a farm. Climb a stone stile, walk between the farm buildings, go through a gate and continue along the right edge of a field. Look out for where a yellow waymark directs you to turn right over a stone stile, turn left to continue along the left edge of a field and climb a stile in the corner.

Keep ahead through rough pasture, climb a ladder stile, bear slightly left across the next field and climb a stile on the edge of Forerigg Wood. Continue through this narrow belt of trees, climb a stile on the far side and walk along the right edge of a field to a stile. After climbing it, keep ahead across a field and, on the far side, climb another stile and turn left onto the towpath of the Lancaster Canal **F**. Follow it back to Lancaster, a distance of 4 miles (6.4km).

The canal was constructed in 1797 in an attempt to prolong the prosperity of Lancaster by linking it with Preston and the industrial area of south Lancashire. This stretch is particularly peaceful and attractive. Approaching Lancaster, the towpath runs parallel to a road on the left and there are views of the hilltop priory and castle. After passing under bridge 98, turn left up to a road **G**, turn sharp left to cross the bridge, turn left again and continue along the other side of the canal. Just before the next bridge, go up a sloping paved path, turn left to cross the bridge **H** and keep ahead along Penny Street into the town centre. Turn left by Waterstone's bookshop and turn right into Castle Hill to return to the start.

Anglezarke, White Coppice and Great Hill

Start	Anglezarke car park, signposted from minor road between Belmont and Rivington
Distance	9 miles (14.5km)
Approximate time	5 hours
Parking	Anglezarke car park
Refreshments	None
Ordnance Survey maps	Landranger 109 (Manchester, Bolton & Warrington), Explorer 287 (West Pennine Moors)

The route is mainly through woodland, beside reservoirs and across open moorland and there are a series of superb and extensive views. Soon after the start it passes by White Coppice, where the cricket ground is generally considered to be the most picturesque in Lancashire, and towards the end goes through Lead Mines Clough, of great interest to those keen on industrial archaeology. This is a lengthy but not difficult walk. There are, however, some potentially wet and muddy moorland paths and it would be best to choose a fine and reasonably clear day.

Great Hill

From the car park, go through a kissing gate and take the tarmac path signposted 'Anglezarke Trail'. The path goes through trees and bracken, passes below a quarry face and descends to a T-junction. Turn right beside an arm of Anglezarke Reservoir, like the neighbouring Yarrow Reservoir one of a chain constructed in the area during the Victorian era for Liverpool Corporation. The path climbs through attractive woodland, bends first left and then sharply right and continues uphill, passing to the left of High Bullough Reservoir. Go through a kissing gate, keep ahead and, at the end of the reservoir, turn right down to another kissing gate. After going through that one, walk along an undulating wooded path, climb a stile, continue above Anglezarke Reservoir, climb another stile and head through trees and bracken, later descending steps and climbing a stile onto a lane Ⓐ.

Turn left, at a public footpath sign turn right through a kissing gate and walk along a track. After the next stile, the track keeps along the base of cliffs to reach a kissing gate on the left. A short detour through the gate and across a bridge over The Goit leads to the pretty hamlet of White Coppice, a

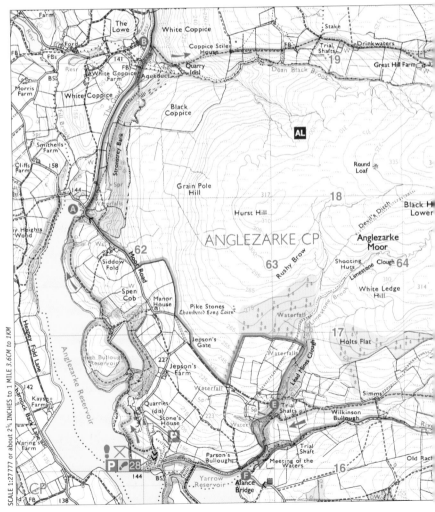

SCALE 1:27 777 or about 2¼ INCHES to 1 MILE 3.6CM to 1KM

collection of stone cottages overlooking a cricket field. Weaving, farming and quarrying were once the main sources of employment here.

The main route continues ahead, climbing along a cobbled track to a footpath sign to Belmont Road and Brindle. Turn sharp right Ⓑ to follow a clear path over the open and bleak expanses of Anglezarke Moor, passing several ruined farms. After climbing steps to a T-junction, turn right along a track which continues steadily up to a

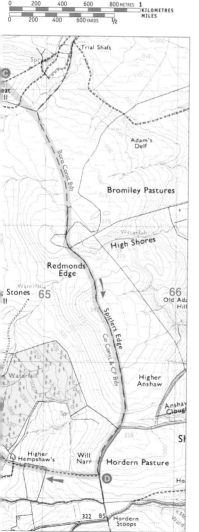

stile. Climb it and head up to the well-constructed cairn on the summit of Great Hill, 1250 ft (381m) high and a superb all-round viewpoint Ⓒ.

Just before reaching the summit you join a slabbed path and then continue along it as it turns right to head across the moorland in the direction of the Winter Hill television transmitter, seen on the horizon. Climb a stile in a dip and continue along this slabbed path – a boon for walkers in such boggy and badly-drained terrain – which winds up and down along Spitler's Edge. After the path ends, continue along a stony path, initially to the left of a broken-down wall and then crossing the wall to pick up a clearer path along its right side. Climb a stile, keep ahead, later descending sharply into a dip, and walk about 400 yds (365m) before reaching the Belmont-Rivington road. Turn right here Ⓓ onto a straight and grassy path.

At first the path runs along the top of a low embankment. Pass through a wall gap, keep above a ditch on the right, go through another wall gap and pass to the the left of a ruined farm to join a track. Walk along this clear and winding track to a ladder stile and, after climbing it, keep ahead and turn right to climb another one. Turn sharply left Ⓔ and head down into Lead Mines Clough, mined from at least the 17th century up to 1837 and containing some interesting and atmospheric remains. On the hill to the right is the Wellington Bomber Monument, a memorial to six airmen who were killed here in 1943 when their plane crashed on a training flight.

Keep beside a stream on the right, cross a bridge and continue first along the right side of the stream and later alongside Yarrow Reservoir to a gate. Go through onto a lane Ⓕ which leads back to the start.

Further Information

 ## The National Trust

Anyone who likes visiting places of natural beauty and/or historic interest has cause to be grateful to the National Trust. Without it, many such places would probably have vanished by now.

It was in response to the pressures on the countryside posed by the relentless march of Victorian industrialisation that the trust was set up in 1895. Its founders, inspired by the common goals of protecting and conserving Britain's national heritage and widening public access to it, were Sir Robert Hunter, Octavia Hill and Canon Rawnsley: respectively a solicitor, a social reformer and a clergyman. The latter was particularly influential. As a canon of Carlisle Cathedral and vicar of Crosthwaite (near Keswick), he was concerned about threats to the Lake District and had already been active in protecting footpaths and promoting public access to open countryside. After the flooding of Thirlmere in 1879 to create a large reservoir, he became increasingly convinced that the only effective way to guarantee protection was outright ownership of land.

The purpose of the National Trust is to preserve areas of natural beauty and sites of historic interest by acquisition, holding them in trust for the nation and making them available for public access and enjoyment. Some of its properties have been acquired through purchase, but many of the Trust's properties have been donated. Nowadays it is not only one of the biggest landowners in the country, but also one of the most active conservation charities, protecting 581,113 acres (253,176 ha) of land, including 555 miles (892km) of coastline, and over 300 historic properties in England, Wales and Northern Ireland. (There is a separate National Trust for Scotland, which was set up in 1931.)

Furthermore, once a piece of land has come under National Trust ownership, it is difficult for its status to be altered. As a result of parliamentary legislation in 1907, the Trust was given the right to declare its property inalienable, so ensuring that in any subsequent dispute it can appeal directly to parliament.

As it works towards its dual aims of conserving areas of attractive countryside and encouraging greater public access (not easy to reconcile in this age of mass tourism), the Trust provides an excellent service for walkers by creating new concessionary paths and waymarked trails, maintaining stiles and foot bridges and combating the ever-increasing problem of footpath erosion.

For details of membership, contact the National Trust at the address on page 95.

 ## The Ramblers' Association

No organisation works more actively to protect and extend the rights and interests of walkers in the countryside than the Ramblers' Association. Its aims are clear: to foster a greater knowledge, love and care of the countryside; to assist in the protection and enhancement of public rights of way and areas of natural beauty; to work for greater public access to the countryside; and to encourage more people to take up rambling as a healthy, recreational leisure activity.

It was founded in 1935 when, following the setting up of a National Council of Ramblers' Federations in 1931, a number of federations earlier formed in London, Manchester, the Midlands and elsewhere came together to create a more effective pressure group, to deal with such problems as the disappearance and obstruction of footpaths, the prevention of access to open mountain and moorland and increasing hostility from landowners. This was the era of the mass trespasses, when there were sometimes violent

Leighton Hall and Morecambe Bay

confrontations between ramblers and gamekeepers, especially on the moorlands of the Peak District.

Since then the Ramblers' Association has played an influential role in preserving and developing the national footpath network, supporting the creation of national parks and encouraging the designation and waymarking of long-distance routes.

Our freedom to walk in the countryside is precarious and requires constant vigilance. As well as the perennial problems of footpaths being illegally obstructed, disappearing through lack of use or extinguished by housing or road construction, new dangers can spring up at any time.

It is to meet such problems and dangers that the Ramblers' Association exists and represents the interests of all walkers. The address to write to for information on the Ramblers' Association and how to become a member is given on page 95.

Walkers and the Law

The average walker in a national park or other popular walking area, armed with the appropriate Ordnance Survey map, reinforced perhaps by a guidebook giving detailed walking instructions, is unlikely to run into legal difficulties, but it is useful to know something about the law relating to public rights of way. The right to walk over certain parts of the countryside has developed over a long period, and how such rights came into being is a complex subject, too lengthy to be discussed here. The following comments are intended simply as a helpful guide, backed up by the Countryside Access Charter, a concise summary of walkers' rights and obligations drawn up by the Countryside Agency (see page 94).

Basically there are two main kinds of public rights of way: footpaths (for walkers only) and bridleways (for walkers, riders on horseback and pedal cyclists). Footpaths and bridleways are shown by broken green lines on Ordnance Survey Pathfinder and Outdoor Leisure maps and broken red lines on Landranger maps. There is also a third category, called byways: chiefly broad tracks (green lanes) or farm roads, which walkers, riders and cyclists have to share, usually only occasionally, with motor vehicles. Many of these public paths have been in existence for hundreds of years and some even originated as prehistoric trackways

Countryside Access Charter

Your rights of way are:

- public footpaths – on foot only. Sometimes waymarked in yellow
- bridleways – on foot, horseback and pedal cycle. Sometimes waymarked in blue
- byways (usually old roads), most 'roads used as public paths' and, of course, public roads – all traffic has the right of way

Use maps, signs and waymarks to check rights of way. Ordnance Survey Pathfinder and Landranger maps show most public rights of way

On rights of way you can:

- take a pram, pushchair or wheelchair if practicable
- take a dog (on a lead or under close control)
- take a short route round an illegal obstruction or remove it sufficiently to get past

You have a right to go for recreation to:

- public parks and open spaces – on foot
- most commons near older towns and cities – on foot and sometimes on horseback
- private land where the owner has a formal agreement with the local authority

In addition you can use the following by local or established custom or consent, but ask for advice if you are unsure:

- many areas of open country, such as moorland, fell and coastal areas, especially those in the care of the National Trust, and some commons
- some woods and forests, especially those owned by the Forestry Commission
- country parks and picnic sites
- most beaches
- canal towpaths
- some private paths and tracks Consent sometimes extends to horse-riding and cycling

For your information:

- county councils and London boroughs maintain and record rights of way, and register commons
- obstructions, dangerous animals, harassment and misleading signs on rights of way are illegal and you should report them to the county council
- paths across fields can be ploughed, but must normally be reinstated within two weeks
- landowners can require you to leave land to which you have no right of access
- motor vehicles are normally permitted only on roads, byways and some 'roads used as public paths'

and have been in constant use for well over 2,000 years. Ways known as RUPPs (roads used as public paths) still appear on some maps. The legal definition of such byways is ambiguous and they are gradually being reclassified as footpaths, bridleways or byways.

The term 'right of way' means exactly what it says. It gives right of passage over what, in the vast majority of cases, is private land, and you are required to keep to the line of the path and not stray on to the land on either side. If you inadvertently wander off the right of way – either because of faulty map-reading or because the route is not clearly indicated on the ground – you are technically trespassing and the wisest course is to ask the nearest

available person (farmer or fellow walker) to direct you back to the correct route. There are stories about unpleasant confrontations between walkers and farmers at times, but in general most farmers are co-operative when responding to a genuine and polite request for assistance in route-finding.

Obstructions can sometimes be a problem and probably the most common of these is where a path across a field has been ploughed up. It is legal for a farmer to plough up a path provided that he restores it within two weeks, barring exceptionally bad weather. This does not always happen and here the walker is presented with a dilemma: to follow the line of the path, even if this inevitably means treading on crops, or to walk around the edge of the field. The latter course of action often seems the best but this means that you would be trespassing and not keeping to the exact line of the path. In the case of other obstructions which may block a path (illegal fences and locked gates etc), common sense has to be used in order to negotiate them by the easiest method – detour or removal. You should only ever remove as much as is necessary to get through, and if you can easily go round the obstruction without causing any damage, then you should do so. If you have any problems negotiating rights of way, you should report the matter to the rights of way department of the relevant council, which will take action with the landowner concerned.

Apart from rights of way enshrined by law, there are a number of other paths available to walkers. Permissive or concessionary paths have been created where a landowner has given permission for the public to use a particular route across his land. The main problem with these is that, as they have been granted as a concession, there is no legal right to use them and therefore they can be extinguished at any time. In practice, many of these concessionary routes have been established on land owned either by large public bodies such as the Forestry Commission, or by a private one, such as the National Trust, and as these mainly encourage walkers to use their paths, they are unlikely to be closed unless a change of ownership occurs.

Walkers also have free access to country parks (except where requested to keep away from certain areas for ecological reasons, e.g wildlife protection, woodland regeneration, etc), canal towpaths and most beaches. By custom, though not by right, you are generally free to walk across the open and uncultivated higher land of mountain, moorland and fell, but this varies from area to area and from one season to another – grouse moors, for example, will be out of bounds during the breeding and shooting seasons and some open areas are used as Ministry of Defence firing ranges, for which reason access will be restricted. In some areas the situation has been clarified as a result of 'access agreements' between the landowners and either the county council or the national park authority, which clearly define when and where you can walk over such open country.

Walking Safety

Although the reasonably gentle countryside that is the subject of this book offers no real dangers to walkers at any time of the year, it is still advisable to take sensible precautions and follow certain well-tried guidelines.

Always take with you both warm and waterproof clothing and sufficient food and drink. Wear suitable footwear, i.e. strong walking boots or shoes that give a good grip over stony ground, on slippery

Worsley

Further Information

Cricket ground at White Coppice

slopes and in muddy conditions. Try to obtain a local weather forecast and bear it in mind before you start. Do not be afraid to abandon your proposed route and return to your starting point in the event of a sudden and unexpected deterioration in the weather.

All the walks described in this book will be safe to do, given due care and respect, even during the winter. Indeed, a crisp, fine winter day often provides perfect walking conditions, with firm ground underfoot and a clarity unique to this time of the year. The most difficult hazard likely to be encountered is mud, especially when walking along woodland and field paths, farm tracks and bridleways – the latter in particular can often get churned up by cyclists and horses. In summer, an additional difficulty may be narrow and overgrown paths, particularly along the edges of cultivated fields. Neither should constitute a major problem provided that the appropriate footwear is worn.

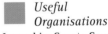

Useful Organisations

Lancashire County Council
Environment Directorate,
PO Box 9, Cross Street,
Preston PR1 8XJ. Tel. 01772 264608

Whalley Abbey

Council for the Protection
of Rural England
25 Buckingham Palace Road,
London SW1W 0PP.
Tel. 020 7976 6433

Countryside Agency
John Dower House,
Crescent Place, Cheltenham,
Gloucestershire GL50 3RA.
Tel. 01242 521381

Forestry Commission
Information Branch,
231 Corstorphine Road,
Edinburgh EH12 7AT. Tel. 0131 334 0303

Long Distance Walkers' Association
Bank House, High Street, Wrotham,
Sevenoaks, Kent TN15 7AE.
Tel. 01732 883705

National Trust
Membership and general enquiries:
PO Box 39, Bromley, Kent BR1 3XL.
Tel. 020 8315 1111
North West Regional Office:
The Hollens, Grassmere, Ambleside,
Cumbria LA22 9QZ. Tel. 08780 6095391

Ordnance Survey
Romsey Road, Maybush,
Southampton SO16 4GU.
Tel. 08456 05 05 05 (Lo-call)

Ramblers' Association
2nd Floor, Camelford House,
87–90 Albert Embankment,
London SE1 7TW.
Tel. 020 7339 8500

Tourist information:
North West Tourist Board
Swan House, Swan Meadow Rd, Wigan
Pier, Wigan WN3 5BB. Tel. 01942 821222

Local tourist information centres:
Accrington: 01254 872595
Blackburn: 01254 53277/681120
Blackpool: 01253 478222
Burnley: 01282 664421
Bury: 0161 253 5111

Clitheroe: 01200 425566
Fleetwood: 01253 773953
Lancaster: 01524 32878
Lytham St Annes: 01253 72560
Manchester (Town Hall):
01612343157/2343158
Morecambe: 01524 582808
Oldham: 0161 627 1024
Preston: 01772 253731
Rawtenstall: 01706 226590/244678
Rochdale: 01706 356592
Salford: 0161 8488601
Wigan: 01942 825677

Youth Hostels Association
Trevelyan House, Matlock, Derbyshire,
DE4 3YH. Tel. 01629 592600
website: www.yha.org.uk

 *Ordnance Survey Maps of
Lancashire*

The area of Lancashire is covered by
Ordnance Survey 1:50 000 ($1\frac{1}{4}$ inches to
1 mile or 2cm to 1km) scale Landranger
map sheets 97, 102, 103, 108, 109 and
Outdoor Leisure maps 2, 7, 21 and 41.
These all-purpose maps are packed with
information to help you explore the area
and show viewpoints, picnic sites, places
of interest and caravan and camping sites.

To examine the area in more detail and
especially if you are planning walks,
Explorer maps at 1:25 000 ($2\frac{1}{2}$ inches to
1 mile or 4cm to 1km) scale are ideal:

21   South Pennines
41   Forest of Bowland & Ribblesdale
276 Bolton, Wigan & Warrington
277 Manchester & Salford
285 Southport & Chorley
286 Blackpool & Preston
287 West Pennine Moors
296 Lancaster, Morecambe & Fleetwood

To get to the Lancashire area use the
Routeplanner Map Great Britain 2002 at
1:625 000 (1 inch to 10 miles or 4cm to
25km) scale or Road Map 4 (Northern
England).

Ordnance Survey maps and guides are
available from most booksellers, stationers
and newsagents.

Index

Entries in *italic type* refer to illustrations